Early Childhood Education Series

Leslie R. Williams, Editor

ADVISORY BOARD: Barbara T. Bowman, Harriet K. Cuffaro, Stephanie Feeney, Doris Pronin Fromberg, Celia Genishi, Stacie G. Goffin, Dominic F. Gullo, Alice Sterling Honig, Elizabeth Jones, Gwen Morgan

(continued)

The

War Play Dilemma

WHAT EVERY PARENT AND TEACHER NEEDS TO KNOW

Second Edition

Diane E. Levin
Nancy Carlsson-Paige

Teachers College, Columbia University
New York and London

Published by Teachers College Press, 1234 Amsterdam Avenue, New York, NY 10027
Copyright © 2006 by Teachers College, Columbia University

Material from Appendix A copyright © 2004 by the American Psychological Association. Reproduced with permission.

Library of Congress Cataloging-in-Publication Data

Levin, Diane E.
The war play dilemma: what every parent and teacher needs to know / Diane E. Levin, Nancy Carlsson-Paige, 2nd ed.
    p. cm. — (Early childhood education series)
    Rev. ed. of: The war play dilemma / Nancy Carlsson-Paige
    Includes bibliographical references and index.
    ISBN 0-8077-4638-X (pbk.)
    1. Play—United States. 2.Children and war—United States. 3. Toys—United States—Psychological aspects. 4. Child development—United States. 5. Teacher-student relationships—United States. I.Carlsson-Paige, Nancy. War play dilemma. II. Title. III. Early childhood education series (Teachers College Press)
LB1137.L55 2005
155.4′18—dc22   2005050096

ISBN-13: 978-0-8077-4638-7 (paper)   ISBN-10: 0-8077-4638-X (paper)

Printed on acid-free paper
Manufactured in the United States of America
13 12 11 10 09 08 07 06   8 7 6 5 4 3 2 1

CONTENTS

PART III: STRATEGIES FOR RESOLVING THE WAR PLAY DILEMMA

PREFACE TO THE SECOND EDITION

AN UNANTICIPATED JOURNEY

The two of us began studying the issue of war play almost 20 years ago. It was part of a larger effort that was already underway: We wanted to learn more about how children make sense of the violence they hear about and see in the world. War play kept getting mentioned when we interviewed parents and teachers about how violence issues came up with children, so we decided to try to explore it further. We had no idea that what we thought was a brief little piece of our larger project on children and violence, would turn into two books in 4 years—the first edition of *The War Play Dilemma* in 1987 and *Who's Calling the Shots?*[1] in 1990—and now, over 15 years later, the second edition of *The War Play Dilemma*. Nor, when we began, did we expect that our own interest in war play, and our appreciation of its importance in many children's lives, would continue to develop and deepen over so long a time.

When we started looking at war play, we had a particular point of view. As early childhood educators, we were coming from a child development tradition. We felt that war play was one valuable way children could use their play to meet their deep developmental needs. Nancy had seen her own sons, who played war and superhero games as children, develop nonviolent attitudes and behaviors as young adults. While we had often limited the play for practical and safety reasons in our own early childhood classrooms, we were not opposed, in principle, to allowing it. And, we didn't need to think about war play much because it wasn't an overriding interest for most of the children.

So when we began with this work on war play, our developmental lens kept us from fully hearing the many parents and teachers who were expressing concern that war play and war toys might be contributing to harmful attitudes about violence in their children. We even turned a deaf ear to what we came to realize was a growing urgency and concern being expressed by parents and teachers about changes in the war play they were seeing. Finally, after about a year of hearing these concerns, we realized that we needed to pay closer attention to what teachers and parents were saying, namely, that more children were more obsessed with war play than in the past. Also, they were saying that it was getting harder to enforce the bans on war and weapons play that had worked successfully before.

Deciding to undertake a brief project to try to understand better why we were hearing so many confusions and concerns, we began collecting data. We used questionnaires and conducted interviews with a wide range of parents and teachers. We also observed children and interviewed several about their play. As we did, we were not prepared for the degree to which almost everyone involved with children wanted to talk about war, weapons, and superhero play, or for the number of strong opinions and concerns we would hear.

Our surprise increased when we traced the concerns we were hearing to a recent rapid transformation in childhood media and toys that seemed to have been going on almost unnoticed. Namely, children's television had been deregulated by the Federal Communications Commission (FCC) in 1984, a year before we began hearing the voices of concern. As a result of deregulation, television programs and toys could be marketed together for the first time. Using television to market toys to children became big business. Almost overnight a large part of the toy market became highly realistic toys linked to children's TV programs. And many of those programs and toys were violent.[2]

We began to wonder whether the growing concerns about war play we were hearing from teachers and parents were connected, at least in part, to children's increased exposure to violent media and media-linked toys. Perhaps they were encouraging children to play out the violent scripts they were seeing on the screen. If this conclusion was correct, then what did it mean for children's war play, what they were learning from it, and how we should deal with it? The 1987 edition of *The War Play Dilemma* was our effort to reassess how adults should deal with children's war play in light of this changing childhood media and play culture.

THE JOURNEY CONTINUES

Since the deregulation of television in the mid-1980s, there has been a steady increase in children's exposure to violence in the media and in their childhood culture. The patterns of marketing to children through the media have continued to escalate and become more sophisticated. Media cross-feeding with TV programs, movies, computer and video games, and whole lines of products linked to the media that are marketed to children increasingly has permeated children's environment. And today, in addition to all of the entertainment violence children see on the screen, they also are exposed regularly to violence in the news, as we found out firsthand after September 11, 2001, when parents and teachers alike described how aspects of that tragic event entered into children's play.

In addition, since the first edition, parents, teachers, and children have taught us a great deal more about how violent media and media culture are affecting children and their war play. What we have learned has led us to decide that it's time to revisit and rethink "the war play dilemma" in light of the current situation.

We realized in the course of writing the first edition of this book that there is no one perfect solution to the war play dilemma but that there is a lot we can do to help children, parents, and teachers work on the problems raised by the dilemma. We still think this is true. This new edition represents the next step in our search to find effective responses to children and their war play in today's world, as we also think about how we can change the world to make it a less toxic environment for children.

We divide this edition into three sections. Part I, "Setting the Stage," provides background information about children's war play and the media culture of today that will help you better understand the issues we need to address if we are going to understand the war play dilemma and develop effective strategies for dealing with it. Part II, "Understanding the War Play Dilemma," closely examines the two seemingly opposite approaches to war play that predominate discussions about it—namely, allowing or banning it. We discuss why neither approach can work very well in today's world and why new ways of thinking about war play are needed. Finally, Part III, "Strategies for Resolving the War Play Dilemma," explores the options available to us for dealing with war play in light of children's needs and current societal influences. Here we offer a wide range of guidelines and strategies for resolving the war play dilemma as best we can in today's world.

We have included three appendices for readers who would like further information on the topic of war play and related issues. Appendix A is a handout with questions and answers on war play that teachers and parents can use for workshops in schools, child care centers, and similar settings. Appendix B consists of two war play-related curriculum webs that show an approach to help teachers plan and keep track of curriculum. Appendix C contains annotated lists of resources for parents and teachers: further readings, organizations working on war play and media-related issues, videos and DVDs for adults on subjects that relate to war play, and children's books that deal with war play and related topics.

Acknowledgments

It was teachers and parents of young children who first led us into the war play dilemma 20 years ago. Because they raised their concerns about children's war play so consistently in the mid-1980s, we came to realize that an important change in society—one that was profoundly affecting children—had taken place. Since then we have continued to learn from the countless teachers and parents who have answered our questionnaires and shared their ideas so freely with us. So much of what we have learned has come from their insights and experience. So our first thanks go to all of the parents and teachers who have taught us so much over the years.

Many parents and teachers spoke to us in anonymous questionnaires or at conferences and workshops. So while we are unable to list all of their names, their voices are ever present in this book and for that we are deeply grateful. Other parents and professionals gave generously of their time for interviews, consultations, and classroom visits. Among them we would like to thank: Betty Jane Adams, Bev Bruce, Farr Carey, Jane Richardson Floyd, Lori Churchill, Martha Eshoo, Christine Gerzon, Kelly Kachinski, Judy Klein, Pamela Linov, Lisa Long, Mary Mayshark-Stavely, Elizabeth Powers, Deborah Rollins, Dawn Rouse, Debra Scavuzzo, Claire Semler, and Dana Vela.

We also have had many colleagues who have contributed to our understanding of the issues discussed in this book and who helped us decide to try to do something about them. First and foremost are the Steering Committee members of Teachers Resisting Unhealthy Children's Entertainment (TRUCE), an organization Diane helped found 10 years ago to work on the issues raised in the first edition of *The War Play Dilemma*. Special thanks go to current members, Jennifer Ablard, Laurel Felt, Marissa Golden, Sarae Pacetta, Kathy Roberts, Janet Schmidt, and Honey Schnapp, for their devotion to helping parents and professionals counteract the harm caused to children by today's violent media culture. We also thank our special colleagues in Concerned Educators Allied for a Safe Environment (CEASE) who have unfailingly supported efforts to resolve the war play dilemma in their work with children as well as in the wider world. And we would like to acknowledge our appreciation for the work and commitment of Daphne White, who for many years headed the Lion and Lamb Project, an organization devoted to reducing the marketing of war toys to children. We continue to appreciate colleagues Mieko Kamii and Karen Worth who made important contributions to our early thinking about the war play dilemma.

Thanks also go to Wheelock College and to Lesley University and the Center for Peaceable Schools at Lesley (where we are both Research Associates) for creating an environment that has always valued the work that we do together. And we offer a sincere thank you to the family of Zell Draz for continuing to support our work in her memory.

The research and writing that have gone into this book represent a truly collaborative endeavor between the authors that has lasted for more than 2 decades. To each other we wish to express warmth and appreciation for the rich and fulfilling experience that this project has provided.

At the heart of all of the ideas in this book are children. We are grateful to all of the children who accepted our presence in their classrooms, ignored our notebooks and tape recorders, and just went on playing. Thanks also go to the many others who answered our questions about their play so willingly. To our own children—despite all the years that have passed, we still can remember warmly "Spider-Man," his costume designer, and "Monster Frog" who helped us to appreciate more deeply the power of play in children's lives—we express special gratitude. And to Jack and Miles, we thank you for helping to keep our ideas fresh and relevant in today's media climate. It is to all of these children that this book is dedicated.

The

War Play Dilemma

WHAT EVERY PARENT AND TEACHER NEEDS TO KNOW

Second Edition

PART I

SETTING
THE
STAGE

1

War Play Under Fire:
Concerns About War Play Today

War play has been around for a long time—artifacts of what might be war toys have been found from ancient Egypt and the Middle Ages. But war play today exists in a context that is very different from any in times past. In the past 20 years, societal forces in the form of television, toys, films, video games, and products have become major influences shaping children's war play.

Before the mid-1980s, the war play children engaged in grew primarily out of their own experience and personal needs. But after the broadcasting industry was deregulated in 1984, this all changed. With deregulation, product-based shows became legal—it became possible to sell toys and products linked to television shows—and advertising time became unrestricted. The toy and television industries quickly joined together to market to children toys directly linked with cartoon programs. They developed whole lines of toys that children could use to act out what they saw on the screen. By December 1985, nine of the ten best-selling toys had television shows connected to them; and in Fall 1987, 80% of all children's television programming was produced by toy companies.

Teachers and parents quickly began to see how the changed marketing practices directed at children were affecting children's play and behavior. Educators, especially those who had worked with children for a long time—whether they had allowed or banned war play—began to express concerns about the war play they were seeing.

Those who traditionally had allowed war play said that children's play was becoming very repetitive. They described how children seemed to get stuck repeating the same play behavior over and over, as if by rote, rather than elaborating their play over time. They described children as assuming the roles of characters they had seen on television, often playing out scenes that resembled television scripts. These play scenarios often used simple static themes and a lot of aimless running around combined with aggressive "macho" and stylized actions.

As one school director with a developmental perspective told us:

> I got divorced when my son was 2 years old. From an early age he loved all kinds of weapons and superhero play. I always felt that he needed it—that it was providing him with a way to express his anger and to feel in control of his life. I figured other children had their own needs that were met in the play. But now I watch the "battle" play at my center, and it really concerns me. The kids do the same things over and over; it doesn't seem to be getting anywhere. They often run around saying "pow" or "bang, bang" with no real purpose. It just doesn't feel right.

Many who tried to ban the play also were concerned about the changes they were seeing after deregulation—particularly a dramatic increase in the levels of aggression and violence. They said it seemed to spread out beyond the war play and permeate more and more children's play of all kinds. Many children were not distinguishing between pretending to hurt someone and actually hurting someone; and when some children did hurt another child, they either did not realize it or resisted taking responsibility for it. Finally, the characters they were modeling themselves after were increasingly of the militaristic type taken directly from television. In the words of one teacher of 3-year-olds:

> I do not permit war play in my classroom, but it sure feels like it's there. Some of the kids find ways to bring it into anything. One boy got red paint on his hands and went around threatening the other children with "blood from where he was shot." Another child, with no warning, started crashing into children [who were] playing ball, saying he was "Rambo." In the house area recently, three children tore the head off of the teddy bear. All they could tell me was that the bear was the "bad guy." They can't seem to get war play out of their minds.

The concerns that teachers expressed after deregulation in the 1980s have continued to the present. The FCC has continued to allow an almost unrestricted climate friendly to broadcasters and to the media and toy industries. As a result, during the decades since deregulation even more changes have taken place in the social climate influencing war play, most of them detrimental to children's healthy play. These are described at greater length in Chapter 2.

Major media conglomerates increasingly have consolidated since the 1980s, making it easier to market all kinds of media and products to children. Films, television shows, videos, video and computer games, toys, products, and fast food chains often join together to market one storyline to children. The problems that began in the 1980s continue to be described by teachers and parents today, but now they often include new problems and a heightened sense of worry and concern. Several factors seem to be contributing to the growing difficulties adults say they are having currently as they try to find approaches to war play.

TENSIONS IN EARLY CHILDHOOD SETTINGS

Many teachers today find themselves dealing with problems whenever children become involved with war play. Conflicts occur with greater frequency in war play than in other kinds of play. Some children, primarily boys, seem to get obsessed with the play and try to bring the themes of the play to other aspects of the classroom.

In 2003, about a year after the United States invaded Iraq, a teacher reported that she was having a very hard year (something we heard from many teachers during that time). She told us a major reason for her difficulty was the war play of her 4-year-old boys.

> This whole school year all but one of the boys in my class has been obsessed with war play. They play some variation of the same theme over and over—there's a bad guy, he needs to get killed. Wherever they play, at the water or sand table, with Lego and blocks, even in the dramatic play area, they designate another child or object as the "bad guy" and then pretend to attack. I have tried to guide them away from the killing and so now they sometimes designate a "jail" and put the bad guy there. I've also gotten it enough in control so that it's rare that anyone gets hurt anymore. I know that's something. But I've had a very hard time getting them to do much of anything in their play but obsess about bad guys.

Regardless of whether they have allowed or banned war play, teachers and caregivers say that it is too often an issue of tension and struggle with children, colleagues, and parents. We have heard this from teachers of children as young as 2 years old.

Many of those who adhere to the "sociopolitical" view, who have always banned war play, say banning no longer works the way it did in the past. Some say they have to repeat their "no guns" and "no pretend fighting in school" rules with increasing frequency. As one teacher told us:

I have taught for 15 years and always had the policy that children put their real or pretend guns in their pocket because "we can't use our guns at school, they can hurt people." We want them to know that even pretending to hurt others is not okay. I still have the rule . . . but it feels like I must state it two or three times as often as a few years ago. I'm really losing my patience.

Other teachers who routinely ban war play describe children sneaking under the slide to pull out a gun or finding ingenious ways of getting around the "no guns in school" rule. For instance, one child took a bite out of a cracker and held it like a gun with his pointer finger, pulling the trigger where the cracker was bitten away. When the teacher reminded him, "no guns in school," he turned the cracker and said it was not a gun but rather the letter "L." Some teachers experiencing this kind of problem say they worry about children learning to sneak around and lie to adults at such a young age.

Those teachers who have felt it is all right to allow war play, with clear structure and limits (e.g., it's okay on the playground, but with no "real" guns), say that the play now seems to easily get out of control, children get hurt with increasing frequency, and it stretches their management skills to new levels. Here's one example:

I have always allowed a limited kind of war and superhero play in the dramatic play area, without toy guns (we call them "real guns"). I'm beginning to question this. A child will bring in a toy "laser" and ask if it's okay because "it's not a gun." A group will get so involved in the play that they zoom out of the block area pretending to shoot or karate chop [like Mighty Morphin Power Rangers] everyone in the room. I have to devote so much of my energy to explaining rules and controlling the play that I'm beginning to wonder if I should ban it completely.

Whether teachers allow or ban war play, we hear other kinds of concerns from them, too. For instance, some describe the trouble many girls have playing with boys who are engaged in war play. They say that the gender divisions between girls and boys in their classrooms are greater, and the boy–girl friendships fewer.

Especially since September 11, 2001, teachers say they have seen increasing incidents of children bringing into their play the violence they hear about in the news. Teachers also mention the presence of violent content from TV shows, films, and video games in children's war play and the influence of realistic toys that are linked to the media. Some wonder whether it is important to distinguish between play that is linked to "entertainment" violence like superhero cartoons and that linked to real-world violence. They wonder how children, who do not make tidy distinctions between what is pretend and what is real, make sense of these different forms of violence when they play.

We hear about ongoing disagreements among teachers and caregivers about the war play policies they should adopt in their classroom or school. The following example captures the kind of problems teachers report:

> My co-teacher and I are having a lot of trouble with each other finding an approach to war and superhero play that we can agree too. She really hates seeing children pretend to hurt each other and wants to impose an out-and-out ban. I see children obsessed with it and want to try to help them deal with that. We are dealing with the children differently. I think it's making for a lot of tension in the classroom.

Teachers who continually try to adapt their war play policies often find persistent and creative resistance from children on an ongoing basis, leading them at times to begin criticizing parents. They ask why parents are allowing their children to be exposed to inappropriate violence in media and toys.

TENSIONS AT HOME

When we queried parents through questionnaires and individual interviews, their responses revealed that teachers were not alone in their discomfort and confusion about war play. Many parents of young children, especially boys, are saying that war play is an ongoing and growing source of tension between themselves and their children. Many voice a sense of confusion; some say they feel out of control. And some parents seem resigned to having a limited ability to influence or limit their children's involvement in war play. We are used to hearing such views of alienation from parents of adolescents, but it is not what we usually expect to hear from the parents of preschoolers.

We asked parents why they thought war play is such a stressful issue for their children and themselves. They responded with a long list of reasons. They pointed to changes in society—television and other media, increased advertising, toys and other products marketed through the media—as major contributors to their difficulties. They voiced concerns about the violence that society now presents to their children—both in entertainment and real-world violence—and how hard it is to avoid.

They said that they could not turn on the television, visit children at other homes, or go to a supermarket, toy store, or playground with their children without encountering some reminder of war and superhero and weapons play.

Many parents expressed consternation about their children's seemingly insatiable desire for an endless array of toys and other products related to violent themes in the media, as well as about the amount and kind of aggression they often observed in their children's play. Often they pointed to the peer group at school as a major source of their children's interest in war play and sometimes blamed teachers for allowing the play in school. Many parents also said that war play was a topic that they often discussed among friends and relatives who have children and with their children's teachers and child care providers.

This response from the parent of a 6-year-old boy reflects many of the issues parents expressed.

> Gary learned about war play in the neighborhood when he was about 3. I tried to ban the violent TV shows and toys in our home, but his grandparents gave him a toy gun and a superhero action figure when he was 4. We always have struggles at toy stores for more of those toys. And, when I ask him not to watch the TV shows at home, he'll watch them at a neighbor's or friend's house. It all makes me feel I have no control. I'm afraid I end up getting "out of control" myself. I yell and get angry. This doesn't help. All of his friends do it [war play]. I often feel I can't do anything about it. I don't know where to turn.

Finally, several parents described how the tension in their relationships with their children crept into their relationships with other adults. Below, a mother, who started out in the "sociopolitical" camp, describes the degree to which emotions, personal and political beliefs, and concerns for children can all contribute to the "dilemma" about war play many parents are experiencing.

> The struggle between my husband and myself over our 8-year-old son's interest in war and superhero play has been growing. Jack seems to be "obsessed" with it. He spends endless hours making drawings of battle scenes, with detailed military bombers, missiles, and guns [which he sees on news programs and in newspaper photos]. He also draws make-believe superhero characters he sees in TV cartoons, video games and movies. He wants camouflage clothes and GI Joe and superhero toys. We will not buy these things for him, but he can do what he wants with his allowance.

When Jack first expressed interest in toy guns at 3 years old, my husband and I agreed we wouldn't allow guns in our home. We wanted Jack to learn that guns and violence were offensive to us, even in "play." We were uncomfortable watching the play shooting and killing and felt responsible to teach our values to Jack.

We found it very hard to hold to our position on this. Jack made guns out of anything—his finger, clay, paper clips. He kept asking for guns and other war toys from grandparents and Santa Claus. They were the first toys he always ran to at friends' houses. The attraction of the war toys seemed much more powerful than our explanations of why his friends could have them but he couldn't.

We gradually realized we could not totally stop this play, despite our efforts. At my urging, we finally decided to give Jack a toy gun. We were making it into a real power struggle with him. I decided that one gun, used with careful limits and a lot of communication about our values, would be a better compromise. I guess I hoped that it would lead to a decrease in his interest in guns and war play.

However, things didn't go as I had hoped. With time, Jack seemed to get more and more involved with the play until now it seems like one of his major interests. We gave in more and more but always with discomfort and ambivalence, especially on my husband's part. He never agreed with allowing the play but didn't have any very helpful ideas about what we should do, so he went along with me. We now are in real conflict. He is convinced we are creating a soldier and warmonger and is feeling trapped by Jack and me. I still feel that his play and war drawings tap into some basic needs Jack has, and I can't see treating this completely differently from how we respond to his other interests. I'm still not sure why it's such a passion for him and wonder if it points to some emotional needs that aren't being met. But, I also see he isn't an overly aggressive or mean child. He seems to care about others.

TENSIONS SPILL OUT BEYOND THE CLASSROOM AND HOME

Occasionally, the problems and concerns created by war and superhero play take on a life bigger than the adults and children directly involved, and sometimes with disturbing consequences in the wider community. Such situations illustrate how different adults' and children's points of view can be on the subject of "pretend" violence. When we hear these stories, we realize with new urgency just how important it is to understand war and superhero play more deeply, and to devise strategies for dealing with it that take that deeper understanding into account. Here is one example that we found especially salient.

> I am a veteran director of a large child care and after-school center. We recently experienced a situation that leaves me searching for help. A 6-year-old boy told another child that he "was going to shoot her." This inappropriate comment was discussed with the two children in what seemed like an appropriate and constructive manner. The day progressed without further incident. But the threatened child went home and told her parents, who made a police report the next day.
>
> A full police investigation ensued. Our center has been chastised by both the parents and the police for not having a policy on "verbal threats," which we now need to develop. I have called the other preschools and public schools in our community, but have yet to find any information or policies that address the issue of verbal threats with sensitivity to a child's developmental progression. What policy will allow for redirection of the dreaded "Lego guns" or the toddler that chews her graham cracker into a gun shape and says "Pow, Pow, You're dead!" to her teacher or a child.[1]

The above situation reached out into the wider community and leads to the realization that war play can create problems that go beyond the children and adults immediately involved.

The next situation, which comes from a worried parent of a 6-year-old, stayed within the boundaries of the school community. But it also shows the potentially harmful directions in which war play can lead children in their interactions with others. It begins to sound very much like the accounts we now hear with increasing frequency of bullying among younger and younger children.

> I have a question about a line of toys made by Lego called "Alpha Team." They are a series of kits with Lego pieces and you follow the directions to make various characters that are designated as "good" or "bad" guy figures. I always think of Lego as being an educational, free-play construction toy. But now I think they are just like ready-made action figures you can buy at the store, which we never bought for our son Derrick.
>
> Now the Alpha Team figures have led to trouble on the playground for Derrick and his friends as they act out the characters. They have decided that in order to be "good guys," there needs to be a "bad guy." They choose an unsuspecting kid on the playground to be the "bad

guy" and then they (the "good guys") attack him. The "bad guy" ends up in tears and my son and his friends end up at the principal's office for "bullying." When there they keep trying to explain that they were just "pretending" to be "good guys"! This has happened three times in the past month and now the parents have been called in for a conference. I am really struggling to figure out what role the toys might be playing in this problem, which is a new one for us. I thought about taking the toys away, but I worry that the damage has already been done and that won't stop the play.

As parents struggle to understand and deal with war play issues, all too often they are told that if they could "just say no" the play wouldn't be such a problem. But one director of a child care center does a very thoughtful job of capturing why parents of today can't do the job on their own.

I don't envy the parents and teachers of today's children. I am a pacifist, and when I was the parent of a young child and first started teaching, I didn't permit war or weapons play at home or school. Most children accepted this easily. Now, my son shares my political attitudes. He has been trying to prevent war play in his home with his 6-year-old son. He tells me that it's a constant struggle. All of his child's environment—his friends, the toys they play with, television programs, and ads—is permeated with aggression and violence, which keep erupting in his play. The teachers and many of the parents at my school tell me the same thing. They don't know what to do inside the classroom or at home to stop this play.

In sum, parents and educators holding either view are concerned because children's war and superhero play has become a source of tension in their relations with children. They say that

- They are seeing a greater influence of television and other media on children's war play.
- Children seem to be increasingly obsessed with war play.
- More and more toys are linked to violent media, and these are harder and harder to keep out of children's reach.
- It is more difficult to allow and manage, or to ban, war play.
- When war play occurs, more children get hurt.
- War play is invading the curriculum in ways that are eroding the teachers' sense of control.

CHANGES IN PLAY

There is yet another factor that has stood out for us more and more in the years since we began studying war play: Adults are no longer concerned just with war and superhero play. Now, we hear from both parents and teachers that they are very worried about changes in children's play in general.

In the words of one very experienced educator who has always tried to put play at the center of the curriculum in her preschool classroom:

> The children's play is not as dimensional or breadthy as it used to be. They do the same thing over and over. They won't try something a lot of different ways; they'll try one thing and then walk away— I mean everybody. They kind of skim along. Some are still okay if you take the time to get them more breadthy, but you'd hope they'd do it themselves. They don't stick with any of it. It's like they keep changing the channels on television. I don't think of this as "Things aren't like they used to be." I have a real kernel of fear inside me about this stuff. Look at how little they are. What are they going to be like when they're 12 years old?

Educators also claim they are seeing more children who do not seem to know how to play. This teacher's comments capture what we have heard from many others.

> I've had to stop having an open-ended playtime in my room. For years I had interest areas where I put out materials that offered lots of possibilities for exploration and play that I thought would interest the children. But it got to the point that when I put out the materials children did not seem to know what to do with them. Many would dabble a bit and either flit to another activity or get into some kind of dispute. Now, I have to provide much more narrowly structured activities at the play areas and then I work real hard trying to help the children gradually learn how to play in a more creative way.

An experience that worried us was our recent return to interview a teacher that Diane had interviewed many years ago about the play in her classroom. Ten years ago, we were greatly impressed by the high quality of creative and elaborated dramatic play this teacher nurtured in the children. It was play that incorporated the issues that were most pressing in the children's lives and in the world around them. When we talked to this teacher for this edition, she said:

Our concern right now is that we are seeing children do a lot of hurtful play. I am spending a lot of time in conflict resolution. And when there is a controversy they are ready to hit. They are ready to name call. This concern has been growing but in the last couple of years it is much more prevalent than before. And, it's a growing problem. Over the last few years it seems like there are more and more and more children involved.

This teacher listed several specific aspects of the play today that were of particular concern.

The children are more aggressive. They are ready to yell at one another. For example, a group of boys that I have are very athletic young boys. And I have no problem with rough and tumble play. I think there is a place for it. But they cannot draw the line between that play and really hurting each other. They will cross the line every time.

Another thing that I have noticed is that the children have a more difficult time distinguishing between real and nonreal. I have some boys who really truly think that The Hulk is real. "When I grow up I am going to be The Hulk," they say. They are going to do whatever he does (I haven't seen it) and they are going to be The Hulk. And Spider-Man. "Spider-Man is a man. I am going to be a man, so therefore I can be Spider-Man."

Another thing about their play is that I don't think it is as sophisticated as it once was. I see more immature kinds of play. They are not able to pretend. All they can do is imitate TV characters. And then, when they try to play using TV characters, they often end up fighting over who can be which character before they even begin to play.

All of this has made we wonder what was being allowed in these children's homes. So one day I asked the children, "Where do you eat dinner?" And I had probably ten who said that they ate alone in their bedrooms in front of the TV. Some of them ate in the den or another room in front of the TV—also alone. And then some of them ate at the table with the TV on. And there may have been one or two who ate at the table with their family and no television. I was very shocked. I was particularly shocked about eating in their bedrooms alone. And the thing about it is, what I see is it's not that the parents don't love and care for their children, they just are not getting it.

We have always tried to work with parents to help them appreciate and promote their children's play. But now I understand much better why they often tell us that their children seem more interested in watching TV or a video, and playing video games, than in engaging in dramatic and creative play in their playrooms full of toys. Parents repeatedly say that when they try to get their children to play, they often seem to quickly lose interest and say they're bored.

Things have changed a lot since I began teaching. I didn't really get it until recently what all these changes mean for children. We need to take more seriously how they are affecting children and try to figure out what we can do to reduce the harmful effects.

It is to these changes and how they impact children and the war play dilemma that we turn in Chapter 2. The chart below summarizes the current concerns of parents and teachers about war play.

Summary of Teachers' and Parents' Concerns About War Play Today

- It is harder to ban than in the past.
- Attempts to ban often lead to children trying to sneak and bypass adult edicts.
- It is harder to allow war play today than in the past because it easily gets out of control and children get hurt.
- More gender divisions occur between girls and boys than in many other forms of play.
- When war play occurs, TV and film characters, plots, and toys heavily script its content.
- More violence from the news is brought into the play.
- Many question whether parents protect their children enough from violent TV content.

2

Childhood Under Fire... and How This Contributes to the War Play Dilemma

Taking a closer look at the popular childhood culture, which literally assaults children with violence on a daily basis, can go a long way toward helping us understand current concerns about the war play of today. At the heart of that culture is the media—television shows, videos and films, computer and video games, and the Internet.

Young children growing up today spend an enormous amount of time consuming media. Two- to seven-year-olds now average over 3 hours a day of "screen time."[1] Furthermore, much of what children see on the screen focuses on violence, both "for fun" violence and violence in the news. And when they are not sitting in front of a screen, children often are involved with media-linked products that reach into more and more aspects of their lives—toys, breakfast cereals, lunchboxes, pajamas, shoes, products for birthday party themes, and link-ups with fast food chains.[2]

MARKETING VIOLENCE TO CHILDREN

In September 2000, the Federal Trade Commission (FTC) published a landmark report showing how the entertainment industry routinely has marketed violent entertainment to children. The report described a host of unethical marketing practices used by the industry to draw children into violent entertainment. For instance, it was found that films were being promoted to children under the ages considered appropriate by the industry's own rating system.

One common approach cited is the marketing of violent toys linked to films rated PG-13 or R to children as young as 4. This was done with violent films such as *Godzilla, Tomb Raider, Spider-Man, Star Wars, Terminator,* and *The Hulk,* to name just a few. The toys developed with films usually are linked also to other media, such as television shows and video games, as well as the hundreds of other products marketed to young children and also linked to the films. It is these violent media and the accompanying merchandising campaigns that draw young children into a culture of violence and are at the heart of the war play dilemma we face.

Violence Sells

As explained earlier, we can trace the increase of marketing violence to children to the deregulation of children's television by the FCC in 1984. With deregulation, violent media became a powerful vehicle for marketing products to children. One violent TV program after another, all linked to whole lines of toys and a growing number of other products, swept through children's popular culture—Masters of the Universe, GI Joe, Teenage Mutant Ninja Turtles, Power Rangers, and most recently professional wrestling, to name but a few of the most successful. The amount of violence increased steadily in the most popular children's television shows. For instance, at the peak of its popularity, each Power Rangers episode averaged about 100 acts of violence, twice as many acts as in the Teenage Mutant Ninja Turtles, which was the previously most successful show.[3] It is now estimated that by the end of elementary school, the average child will have seen 8,000 murders and 100,000 other acts of violence on the TV screen.[4]

Also with deregulation, came a dramatic increase in the use of gender stereotyping to market to children, especially boys. Violence was used to capture the boys' market, while appearance and, increasingly, sex and sexiness were used to capture the girls' market. As discussed in Chapter 3, both boys and girls are susceptible to learning the highly gender-divided messages that the media provide. And the content associated with these divisions between girls and boys has become more and more extreme over time. Following from the tendency for children to focus on the most extreme, most graphic content they can find, industry has found that becoming more extreme is effective marketing. And as we get increasingly desensitized to each new escalation, industry finds it can push the envelope further.

The push to use violence as a tool for selling products to children quickly spread beyond television and films, as described above. About 90% of today's children live in households that own or rent video game players.[5] A 2001 Children Now survey of the content of video games found that over 80% of the games researchers examined contained violence. Children also are increasingly involved with computers and the Internet. Over two thirds of U.S. children have computers at home,[6] a large proportion of which provide access to the Internet and all the violence it contains.

While there are voluntary rating systems for television programs, films, and video games, a 1999 Gallup poll found that 86% of Americans think the amount of violence children see is a serious problem.[7] And a Kaiser Family report released in 2004 concluded:

> Without a doubt, parents are deeply concerned about the impact today's media are having on their children. Parents are very concerned that their children are exposed to too much sexual content, violence and adult language on TV. [8]

Better ways of managing the violent media that get into children's lives are needed, as are controls on the unethical marketing practices identified in the FTC report.

Who's in Control?

But this is an increasingly daunting task. Today, seven major media conglomerates own the bulk of the media we consume and have almost unlimited control over most of the images to which we are exposed and products linked to them. They are free to market their wares to children and use concern for profits as their guiding principle instead of what is best for children.

First Amendment arguments are used regularly as the reason for giving the entertainment industry unlimited freedom to market to children. But these arguments fail to take into account the long history in this country of government protection of children from things that harm them—abuse, tobacco, alcohol, sex, driving cars, factory labor, serving in the military, to name but a few examples. What about the rights of parents and children to live without the pervasive presence in their everyday lives of violent media images that take their toll in so many ways?

In recent years, public criticism about the current situation has grown. For instance, the American Psychological Association issued a position statement calling for federal restrictions on advertising aimed at children under 8 years old.[9] The statement called advertising to young children *exploitative,* citing research showing that children under age 8 do not have the cognitive ability to understand the persuasive intent of ads.

The advertising industry has taken increasingly aggressive steps to try to defuse the possible impact of public criticism. For instance, in January 2005, the Alliance for American Advertising, a national lobby, was created. Its stated purpose is to "defend the industry's First Amendment rights to advertise to children and to promote its willingness to police itself." [10]

More Than Child's Play

There is a growing consensus that the media violence that engulfs many children is harming them. In 2000, six major medical groups—including the American Academy of Pediatrics, the American Medical Association, and the American Psychological Association—issued a statement on the effects of entertainment violence on children.[11] After reviewing hundreds of studies, they concluded that there is a definite connection between media violence and aggressive behavior in children. They also say that some children who watch a lot of media violence become desensitized to violence in real life. And, children exposed to violent media at a *young age* are more likely to engage in violent and aggressive behavior later in life than children who are not exposed.

The current violent media environment can help us understand many of the concerns voiced by parents and professionals, described in Chapter 1, about the amount of war play they are seeing and the children who often seem obsessed with it. This media environment gives children vast quantities of violent content to try to figure out and master. Since play is the primary vehicle that children have available for doing this, we would expect children who are exposed to this onslaught of media violence to engage in more play with violence than children did in the past.

From Toy Story to Toy Nightmare!

The toys linked to violent media also can help explain many of the concerns we hear about the nature of children's war play today. Toys have a very big influence on play. Some kinds of toys tend to promote higher quality play than others. Multipurpose and unstructured toys like clay, blocks, generic toy figures, and baby dolls encourage play that children can control and shape to meet their individual needs. Highly structured or realistic toys, like action figures that are based on TV programs and/or movies, can have the opposite effect. They can take control of play away from children. They channel children into playing particular themes in particular ways. Unlike more open-ended toys that children can use in an endless variety of ways, these toys easily can take control away from children, making it harder for them to shape or define their play according to their own evolving needs.

When children are given highly realistic toys that are linked to the violence they have seen on the screen, they get the message they should use these toys to act out what they have viewed. Furthermore, because these toys are so highly structured, we shouldn't be surprised when we see play that is narrow and repetitive, and stays focused on content and actions that involve violence and pretend fighting. Because of their power to control play and keep it so focused on violent themes, these toys help increase the impact media violence has on younger children. But parents who work very hard to keep these toys from their children's playrooms, face an uphill battle. Violent toys and images linked to them are so all-pervasive in the commercial childhood culture that most parents can't keep them away despite their best efforts.

WHEN THE WORLD IS A DANGEROUS PLACE

In addition to all of the entertainment violence that fuels children's war play, there is also an unprecedented level of real-world violence that enters children's lives through the news—on television and the radio, in graphic photographs in newspapers, and on covers of magazines. Then, children also hear about it in the conversations of adults and even from other children. As with violence in entertainment media, while we can reduce the amount of exposure children have, we cannot fully protect them from it.

What news violence does get in, provides further content to fuel children's play with violence and the issues they need to work on in their play. It can increase children's confusion about what is pretend and what is real. It also contributes to the lessons children learn about the world being a dangerous place.

Another form of violence in children's lives that contributes powerful content for war play is beyond the primary focus of this book—namely, the violence that children experience directly in their own lives. So while the content of this book is relevant for children who have experienced violence directly, there are many other issues that need to be addressed regarding war play when we add real-world violence to the war play equation.

VIOLENCE AND WAR PLAY THROUGH CHILDREN'S EYES

The way young children think and learn influences how they use the violence they see in their play. It also makes them more vulnerable to learning harmful lessons about violence both in and out of their play.

How Young Children Think

There are several special characteristics of young children's thinking that affect how they interpret their experience. Learning to recognize those characteristics can help us better understand why the violence marketed to children is so harmful and unethical.

Young children do *not fully distinguish between pretend and real.* They use what they have learned about good guys and bad guys and about fighting and weapons from a fictional show to interpret what they hear about real-world violence. The fact that a 4-year-old has been told that the Power Rangers are really actors, not soldiers, does not stop him from giving them "real" soldier status.

They focus on the most *dramatic and concrete aspects of the situation*—not the more abstract concepts underlying it. The fighting and weapons are what children gravitate to, not the underlying issues. This is one reason why children are so drawn to violence with all its graphic and salient action; it helps explains why violence "sells" so well.

They *do not make logical causal connections.* As children focus on the action and excitement of the fighting, they do not think about the pain and suffering that might result.

They *focus on only one aspect of the situation at a time.* Children's thinking is more like a series of separate slides rather than like a film. They do not think about the whole picture—the context for the fighting—why there is fighting, or what the possible outcomes are likely to be.

They think in terms of *dichotomous categories.* In fights you either "win" or "lose." There are good guys and bad guys; the Power Rangers are clearly "good," while whomever they are fighting is "bad." Furthermore, anything the "good" side does seems to be unquestionably "right," and what the "bad" side does, "wrong."

How Young Children Learn

Children build ideas about the violence they see and its role in their own lives through a slow process of construction. They don't passively absorb information about violence as it is presented to them. They transform it into something that is meaningful to them. And the meaning they make builds onto what they already have figured out about violence from prior experience.

The way children think and learn makes them especially susceptible to the lessons about violence they see on the screen. For instance, because young children tend to focus on one aspect of a situation at a time and do not connect the scenes of a story into a logical sequence, they often ignore the context in which violence occurs and what happens to a character who commits or is a victim of violence.

Similarly, when children hear something on the news about the United States fighting in Iraq, they might try to figure it out by connecting it to something they already learned about fighting from the Mighty Morphin Power Rangers or Spider-Man. So they might begin using Power Ranger karate chops to try to fight the "bad guy" Iraqis. One mother reported that her 4-year-old son actually asked if there were Power Rangers fighting in Iraq.

THE CHALLENGE FACING ADULTS

As media, with all its violence, have become such a powerful force in children's lives and as the entertainment industry has been given so much power over marketing violence to children, it has become more important now than ever before that we grapple with how to solve the war play dilemma. Clearly, working hard to protect children as much as possible from the onslaught of violence is at the center of our approach.

However, as we heard from the voices of parents and teachers in Chapter 1, such efforts rarely will be enough—it's almost inevitable that we will have to face the war play dilemma. And when we do, understanding the nature of the problem we're up against as well as how children think and learn will be key to helping us resolve the dilemma in children's best interests.

PART II

UNDERSTANDING
THE WAR PLAY
DILEMMA

3

The Great Divide: Examining the Two Sides of the War Play Debate

Can the war play dilemma be resolved in a way that incorporates both points of view about war play—the developmental view, which focuses primarily on the needs of children, and the sociopolitical view, which focuses primarily on what children learn from the play? Does accepting one view necessitate rejecting the other? To answer these questions, let's begin by stepping back and carefully examining the two views in light of our goals for children and what is happening with regard to war play in today's world.

THE DEVELOPMENTAL VIEW: WAR PLAY MEETS CHILDREN'S NEEDS

Underlying the developmental view is the assumption that *play, including war play, is a primary vehicle through which children work on developmental issues.* Is this so, and if it is, how and why is this the case? Is it always the case?

Play and Development

Most proponents of the developmental view focus primarily on children's individual needs and the role of play in helping children meet them. They argue that play is at the root of learning and development. They believe that it is mainly through play that children work out key developmental issues of their age and stage and construct an understanding of concepts and feelings. Children bring their experience into their play, where they work out unique meanings in original ways. As they do, they incorporate new ideas and experiences into their play, and the content of the play gradually evolves and changes as mastery and understanding progress. Thus, the play process supports children's continuous development and learning.

By this argument, for play to serve its optimum function, the origins and themes of play should come from children themselves. Children need to be in charge of what they play; their choices reflect their level of development, experiences, needs, and interests. Therefore, children are the best guides of what they need to work on, when, and how. So, when children choose to engage in war play, even if we would prefer they didn't, they are showing us what they need to work on. As they do, their play is likely to help them work out developmental issues and needs.

Meeting Developmental Needs Through War Play

How can war play help children work on developmental issues and needs? One major task young children face is that of gaining control over their impulses. In war play, children assume the roles of powerful fantasy characters, express aggression in pretend situations, and engage in "pretend fighting," all of which can help them to learn about impulse control as they struggle to stay within acceptable boundaries and receive feedback about their actions from people and objects in their environment.

Young children also are working on constructing boundaries between fantasy and reality. War play provides children with a special forum for understanding this difference because of the dramatic differences between real life and the pretend characters and plots in war play. When children take on familiar roles in dramatic play, it is much more tied to their real experiences than is pretending to be fantastic, imaginary characters. Also, children can experiment with fantasy characters in a variety of situations and find that there are limits that separate real from imaginary. When a child who is pretending to be a "good guy" pushes another child and claims that he did it because he has "super powers," the responses of the other child and nearby adults help him learn that real and pretend are not the same.

Young children gradually are learning to progress beyond egocentrism and to take points of view other than their own. As they take on contrasting roles (e.g., "good guy" vs. "bad guy"), work interdependently with other children in these roles, and see how their actions affect one another, their war play can help them understand different points of view and the rules that govern interactions among people.[1]

Children also are working on developing a sense of their own competence as separate, autonomous people. This can be exciting but at the same time threatening to the young child. The early years are also a time when children first experience separation from home and separation from their primary caregivers. The sense of power and competence that is experienced in war play—as children pretend to be superheroes with super powers, for instance—can help children feel like strong and separate people who can take care of themselves.

Finally, young children are struggling to understand the things they hear about the world around them, and as we saw in Chapter 2, today they are exposed to a great deal of violence. Children can use their war play as one important vehicle for integrating and making sense out of what they have heard. For example, children might see soldiers with guns on the television news and bring this image into their play in an effort to understand it or to make it less scary. They might do similar things when they see an episode of Mighty Morphin Power Rangers or Batman.

It's "Just Pretend"

When we talk to adherents of the developmental view, they usually say that war play is "just pretend" for most children and that it is not connected to "real-world" violence in the child's mind. They point to the fact that, while adults may see connections between the play and violence in society, the content and concepts used in children's war play have a different meaning for children than they have for adults. And as we saw in Chapter 2, children do have their own unique ways of making sense of war play.

Why Is War Play So Appealing?

Based on the discussion so far, we can see that developmental theory points to a variety of ways that war play can help young children work on the issues at their level of development. But this does not necessarily help account for the deep interest many children seem to have in war play. What can account for this "passion"?

First, war play may be a very compelling and deeply satisfying form of play for young children because, perhaps more than most other types of play, it helps them experience power and control. At an age when many of life's experiences can lead to feelings of helplessness and being out of control—for instance, their experiences as they work on the developmental tasks of becoming separate, autonomously functioning individuals—young children are looking for avenues that will help them overcome and progress beyond these feelings.

Second, the content of war play may be especially appealing to young children because of the nature of the thinking that characterizes the early years. Societies have always provided children with much of the content they use in their play; the content for war play that society currently is providing fits neatly with the way children view and interpret their world. They are drawn to the salient perceptual features of things. War and superhero figures provide graphic images for children to use in their play—muscles, ray guns, and explosions. They also tend to think in dichotomous groupings—good or bad, right or wrong, boy or girl— someone cannot be both good and bad simultaneously. Images of war and fighting and superhero images from entertainment media embody many of these "black-and-white" characteristics.

Third, while the basic "cap gun" of the past appealed to young children because of the power and strength it symbolized, many current war toys and toys of violence have even greater appeal. They are designed to attract young children's attention by incorporating characteristics that are especially well matched to several aspects of young children's thinking and interests.

For instance, mechanical toys that can be "transformed" from one thing to another through a sequence of predictable steps (e.g., from an evil robot to a laser bomber plane and back) match children's interests in learning about causality, parts and wholes, and how one object can be two different things at the same time. Similarly, when young children are beginning to work on the transition from static to dynamic thinking—from thinking that is like a series of separate frames of a film to that which is more like a film—transformers provide a very appealing cognitive challenge. In addition, toys that offer the promise of power and strength, and that are "like" characters children actually see performing dramatic feats on television, match children's desire to feel strong, while also providing the concrete and salient images that appeal to children.

Finally, it seems that something about war play is especially well matched to the experiences and developmental issues of boys. Parents and teachers commonly observe that, while some girls are attracted to war play, it is most often boys who show a compelling interest.

Why More Boys Than Girls?

Several arguments are used to explain this gender difference. Some attribute it to sex-role stereotyping children experience from the earliest years. According to this argument, boys are encouraged—by their parents, the toys they are given, and the images and role models they see in their environment—to play in more independent and aggressive, less nurturing ways than girls. From this perspective, the highly gender-divided environment of today greatly amplifies any differences between the play of girls and boys that may be caused by biological and genetic factors.

Another perspective argues that gender differences come from children actively trying to figure out what it means to be a male or a female. According to this view, children learn their gender label— "I am a boy" or "I am a girl"—at about the age of 18 months. Then, they begin to look to the world around them, including their families, preschools, and the media, for information about what boys do and what girls do. As they do this, they are most likely to notice the most salient and graphic differences. And if they see a lot of gender stereotyping, this is what they will learn.

Combining the lenses provided by these two perspectives can help explain how sex-role stereotyping in the environment might lead to boys' greater interest in war play. If children are seeing and experiencing sex-role stereotyping in their environment, it is these images they will use in constructing their understanding of the roles that accompany the gender labels they have learned. As explained in Chapter 2, the very macho, primarily male superhero figures children see in the media, along with the frequent images of "pretty," often highly sexualized females, make the distinction between male and female roles clear and simple. They provide boys with some of the most graphic information for defining male gender roles that is available in their environment.

Many adults question the "macho" attributes these characters embody and feel they are providing boys with undesirable role models. These characters may not be optimal for boys' healthy gender development. At the same time, given that these models do exist, boys may be so attracted to them because they are responding to a genuine need to find clearly defined male models with which to identify. And as long as popular and media culture continues to provide this extreme gender-divided content to girls and boys, and as long as such divisions are highly lucrative for corporations, it is unlikely that we can fully protect children from their influence.

A third interesting explanation for why boys have a greater interest in war play than girls comes from theorists who consider the possibly different courses of development boys and girls go through in the process of achieving gender identification. All children must master the experience of separation from home, but, unlike girls, boys must separate from their primary caregivers, still primarily mothers and other females, and also find male gender models with which to identify. This circumstance puts boys under potentially greater stress than girls, who establish their gender identity by identifying with their primary caregiver. Boys must look for alternative models to their nurturing mothers. It also may create in boys a greater feeling of frustration and anger as they try to move away from their mothers and to find avenues for feeling strong and in control without their mothers. Superhero and war figures offer boys the concrete, powerful models that they are seeking, as well as opportunities to express the possible anger and frustration they are feeling.

Creative Play Versus Imitation

We've now seen that the developmental perspective provides a compelling argument for concluding that war play can serve a positive role in children's development. Children use the *content* of war play to work on the developmental tasks of their stage, including violent content to which they have been exposed in their environment. But for war play to serve this function, children need to be involved in an active *process* over which they are in control—they must determine the script.

At the same time, in recent years we have heard many adults who hold the developmental view begin to voice some uncertainty about it. As we saw in some of the parents' and teachers' discussions of war play cited in Chapter 1, they want to know whether the nature and quality of children's war play can affect the degree to which it meets their needs. And if it can, they wonder whether something is happening to the play now—such as the obsession with violent actions and particular characters, the repetitive and imitative nature of the play, and its lack of variation— to reduce its potential value.

Jean Piaget did significant theoretical work on the value of play.[2] He makes an important *distinction between play and imitation* that can help clarify this issue. For Piaget, when children are involved in creative play, they are in charge of their play—as the scriptwriters, actors, prop people, and the like. In play, children take in information from their experience and use it in their own ways according to their current skills and understandings. On the other hand, when children are engaged in imitation, they are controlled more by external experiences and trying to replicate them. In imitation, children shape their behavior and thinking to external demands. Both play and imitation are essential aspects of development and learning. But Piaget argues that while children initially may imitate some newly observed behavior, play is the central part of the meaning-making process, where children experience mastery and control over experience.

Using the play and imitation lenses to look at war play helps us see that all war play is not the same and some kinds seem to have the potential of meeting children's needs better than other kinds. The degree to which it meets children's needs is affected by the degree to which their activity is primarily play as opposed to primarily imitation.

The descriptions of war play in previous chapters—of children using television-based toys to imitate television images and behaviors in their war play, with little variation, elaboration, or evidence that they are making their own inner meaning from it—sound more like imitation than creative play. Our own surveys showing teachers' concerns with the Teenage Mutant Ninja Turtles and Mighty Morphin Power Rangers confirmed that these forms of war play were more like imitation than play.

When imitation of violence predominates over playing with it and working it through, children's needs probably are not being met as they should be. This can affect such important developmental issues as separation, feelings of power and control, and a sense of mastery of violent content.

Reframing the Developmental View in Today's World

There are definite grounds for the concerns about war play that are voiced by adherents of the developmental perspective. While war play can be a vehicle through which children work on meeting their developmental needs, playing at war does not necessarily ensure that children's needs will be met. The quality and content of the play will affect the degree to which needs are met. If the play is primarily imitative, which seems to be the case for much of the war play today, then the interests of development will not be optimally served by war play.

THE SOCIOPOLITICAL VIEW:
WAR PLAY TEACHES HARMFUL LESSONS

Adherents of the sociopolitical view see children pretending to shoot and kill with an apparent intensity and pleasure that worry them. They wonder what is happening to the peaceful, nonviolent values they are trying to instill in children. They worry about the political and moral lessons children are learning from their war play and ask where this play might lead.

Underlying the sociopolitical view is the assumption that *children learn militaristic lessons about violence and conflict from their war play*—lessons about their political and social world. For instance, it can teach them that violence and hurting others is exciting and fun and is the way to settle disputes. Most proponents of this view worry that because children learn from what they play, they are learning negative lessons when they engage in war play. Thus, they believe that by banning war play, we can protect children from learning harmful lessons about violence that war play can teach.

How valid is this argument? To answer this question we found it helpful to consider how children's political and social thinking develops, both inside and outside of their war play.

Early Political and Moral Learning

Most theorists who discuss political socialization believe that it begins in the early childhood years. According to Easton and Hess:

> Every piece of evidence indicates that the child's political world begins to take shape well before he even enters elementary school and that it undergoes the most rapid change during these years. . . . The truly formative years of the maturing member of a political system would seem to be in the years between three and thirteen.[3]

Children's immediate environment plays a crucial role in influencing the content of early political learning. Parents are seen as central in this process. For instance, research has shown that older children's political attitudes tend to reflect those of their parents more than they do those of other environmental influences. The additional finding that political attitudes change the most up to about the age of 13 and are less subject to change thereafter has led to the argument that special attention should be paid to political education in the early years, including that in the school.[4]

Not Just "Little Adults"

Children's early political and moral ideas are very different from adults'. Children have different ideas about what a country is, what a government is, or what causes fighting between people and countries. These ideas are constructed gradually from children's daily lives as they see and experience good and evil, right and wrong, and the disparities in wealth and power among people. A child might hear the label "America" to define where she lives, and then hear on the television news that America bombed Iraq or provided food for victims of the earthquake and tsunami in Asia. She may conclude that there are some people "we" want to hurt and some people "we" want to help. She may even connect this to ideas about who are friends ("good guys") and enemies ("bad guys").

These early concepts will begin to form before children have much understanding of such formal concepts as governments, democracy, the electoral and law-making processes, or war and peace and relationships among nations. Beginning understandings of these concepts will be influenced by early experiences. For instance, lessons about war and peace will grow out of how children see others in their immediate environment resolving conflicts. Concepts about friends and enemies at the immediate and global level will grow out of such things as children's positive and negative social experiences with peers and their exposure to similarities and differences among people. At the same time, children's ideas also are influenced by what they hear about real conflicts in the news.

The fact that children's early political views can look quite different from those of adults often has led to researchers not recognizing the foundations of political development in children. For instance, Robert Coles, the renowned researcher of children's political development, describes how it took him many years to realize that much of what young children were telling him in interviews about their views of the world revealed a great deal of political understanding about how society and relationships among different groups of people worked.[5]

At the same time, there are many adults who have looked at children's war play and attributed a whole range of political concepts of a militaristic nature to the play, when these concepts were perhaps not present. In both cases, a better understanding of the nature of early political concepts and how they might be reflected in war play could assist all adults in their work with children.

All Play Has Political Content

Because children use their play to make sense of experience and build new ideas, it follows that early political concepts will be built in play. Even in "house" and doll play, political lessons can be learned—for instance, lessons about conflict and conflict resolution as two children argue over wanting the role of "father" and reach a compromise solution.

But it is important to remember that there is not a one-to-one correspondence between the content of children's play and the outside world. Moreover, the meaning the content of play has for children may not match the meaning ascribed to the content by adults. For instance, in war play, what "killing" or being the "good guy" or "bad guy" means to any given child and how these concepts are used will be unique and changing. The same is true for the language children bring to their war play: Words such as "lasers," "nuclear bombs," "the Russians," and "the world" have different meanings for children than for adults.

As with the development of all early concepts, the formation of concepts through play is an ongoing and interactive process. Children get information from the world, play with it, build new meaning, and then bring this new meaning back to the world to be used to interpret new experience. It is in this fashion that children gradually connect the political concepts they construct about the world in play to their growing knowledge of the real world. This is how fantasy and reality can be meshed in young children's minds and how the political concepts constructed in "fantasy" war play can influence how real-world experience is interpreted.

How Pretend Meets Real in War Play

A child may see GI Joe shooting his enemy in a television cartoon program and incorporate this image into play, pretending to shoot a child who is the "bad guy" with a stick. Through this play he will be working on figuring out things about shooting and weapons, "bad guys" and "good guys," conflict, and violence. Some of the meaning of the shooting action in the play will have come from the child's experience prior to seeing G.I. Joe on television, while some will be taken from the shooting image that was seen in the cartoon. Then, when this child sees on the television news that the United States is "shooting" in Iraq, he will interpret it in terms of everything he already knows about shooting, enemies, and conflict, some of which has been constructed in his play. Through this ongoing and interactive process, where new experience continually is connected to prior concepts in war play, children's political concepts gradually develop.

War play is especially well suited for influencing the political and moral ideas children develop. Its very nature and content are permeated with issues of power and conflict, right and wrong, good and evil, safety and danger, and friends and enemies—all of which are basic components of the political world. For instance, as children play out power relationships in their war play, what they learn about power is part of the foundation of later adult understanding of power relations among people, groups of people, and nations. Children learn about friends and enemies as they pretend that an alien space creature attacks their building in the block corner. They learn about power and subservience when a child role-playing "Batman" scares other children as he chases them into a corner. Similarly, rule-governed behavior is better understood as a group of children agree to play a superhero chase game by all adhering to the same set of rules.

Children Play What They See

Children find the content for war play in their homes, schools, and communities; from interactions with peers and viewing the mass media; and from the toys they are given to play with.

There are many accounts, both new and old, of children bringing the violence in the world around them into their play. For instance, Anna Freud documented British children using experiences of the German bombing of Britain in their war play during World War II.[6] Throughout the conflict in Northern Ireland, Catholic children used British soldiers as enemies in their play.[7] Teachers describe Palestinian children on the West Bank re-enacting "bad" Israeli soldiers breaking into their homes. After September 11, 2001, many parents and teachers reported that the enemy in children's play became Osama bin Laden, and then the enemy became Saddam Hussein during the war against Iraq.

There are also many accounts of children bringing content from entertainment violence into their play. Pretending to be Power Rangers, Spider-Man, GI Joe, or professional wrestlers from World Wrestling Entertainment are commonly reported themes. So are fighting games with plots from such films and TV programs as *Star Wars* and *YuGiOh*.

Violence-Saturated Society, Violence-Saturated Play

The environment a society creates for its children shapes the attitudes, values, and behaviors they will develop. As we've seen, whatever content a society provides about violence, conflict and human relationships will affect what its children play and learn.

The content society is providing children today is contributing to the concern often voiced about war play. Despite our best efforts to protect children, as we saw in Chapter 2, they are growing up exposed to a great deal of real violence in their own lives—violence they see and hear about in the news—and fictionalized or entertainment violence on the screen. Thus, they have a great deal of violent content to bring to their play, to work on and learn from.

There is also much political content in what children see on the screen. For example, most animated programs have good guys fighting against bad guys (enemies). The bad guys often are depicted as speaking in unfamiliar, foreign-sounding, and distorted voices and sometimes are faceless and dehumanized. The good guys usually look attractive and appealing, based on mainstream cultural values. Humans are depicted as weak and powerless unless they have machines and an arsenal of weapons to protect them. Children are encouraged to identify with the good guys, who can do whatever violence they want because they are "good," and they always win. The good guys face the constant threat of annihilation unless they remain stronger and better armed than the bad guys. Fighting is glamorized partly because the physical, human pain that results from fighting is almost never depicted. To feel powerful and strong is equated with a sense of well-being.

In addition, there is a lot of information about conflicts and conflict resolution. Disagreements are always terminated by violence; dialogues between "good" and "bad" sides are never depicted, and attempts to understand another's point of view are not portrayed. There is also information about the nature of relationships between males and females. Women generally are depicted in roles that are subservient to men, and often are highly sexualized and the victims of violence.

Then there is also the real-world violence children see in news media. From the point of view of adults, the political content of news violence is not always as black-and-white as it is in violent children's television. However, for children—who focus on one idea at a time and the concrete, most salient aspects of situations—news about real-world violence can convey many of the same political messages as cartoons.

It is all this content about violence that saturates media, as well as seeing how children bring it into their play, that has led many adherents of the sociopolitical view to argue that today's war play is teaching children harmful political and moral lessons.

Finally, the toys a society provides for its children to use in their play can affect what and how they play. Today, as pointed out in Chapter 2, many of the best-selling toys are linked to violent TV, films, and video games. Furthermore, these highly realistic toys almost tell children that when they play they should "imitate" the violence they saw on the screen. It may not be a coincidence that the increased sale of fighting-related toys in the United States often has come at times when government policy is focused on war and increased defense spending.

The Sociopolitical View in Today's World

Applying the sociopolitical lens to the war play of today leads us to conclude that there is legitimate cause for concern about the lessons children can learn from their war play. Children use political content from a variety of sources in their environment to build ideas that are quite different from those of adults. Because play is a primary vehicle for making sense out of experience, children bring what they hear to their play, including war play, and gradually build concepts. As children's exposure to violence increases, they bring more violent content to their play and this affects the lessons they learn. In today's world, we see many children who seem to have a great need to work on violence in their play. In addition, much of the violence children see is connected to entertainment media, where violence is glorified and seen as the method of choice for resolving conflicts. Therefore, the lessons they are learning contribute to their building concepts that glorify and accept violence.

REFRAMING THE WAR PLAY DILEMMA: TWO LENSES ARE BETTER THAN ONE

Our explorations of the two sides of the war play debate have led us to conclude that both sides have a great deal of validity. From the developmental side, children *do* bring to their play what they need to work on. If they bring violent content to their play, than they are trying to meet some need. From the sociopolitical side, children *do* learn from what they play and when they bring violence to their play, they can be learning harmful lessons about violence. So, the dilemma is, how can we reconcile these two seemingly legitimate positions? To answer this question, we have found we need to look at the nature and context of play.

Learning About War and Peace in War Play

All war play is not the same. Is it primarily "play" in which the child controls the content and plot? Or, is it mainly "imitation," where the script is controlled primarily by content from the outside world? The nature, quality, and content of war play affect what it teaches children.

When children are in control of their war play and it grows out of a rich experience base, then they are likely to be active agents in constructing their own political knowledge. When they select those aspects of experience to bring into their dynamic play, they are choosing the information that is most relevant to their needs and political understanding at the moment. When their roles and actions are fluid and changing, their political knowledge is more likely to be expanding, deepening, and advancing. Under such conditions, play is fulfilling its function as a primary vehicle through which children construct concepts. In addition, the basic foundation for later political understanding is being formed in developmentally appropriate ways. As a result, children are likely to bring the political concepts they themselves built in their play, back to their interpretations of and actions in the real world in a meaningful way.

When children are involved in a rich and personally meaningful play process that meets their needs, even when it involves violent content, they can learn political lessons about peace and how to work toward it. But this is not necessarily the case. They also can learn lessons that support militarism and acceptance of violence. Whether these lessons focus primarily on war or primarily on peace will depend on the *total context in which the play occurs.* By "context," we mean such things as the kinds of toys and play materials available to the child, how the violence is resolved in the play, how the child connects the issues worked on in play to the real world, and the role adults play in mediating the lessons that are learned.

But, when war play is dominated by imitation rather than creative play, the political ideas children develop in their play are more likely to be templates of the violence they see than understandings they construct themselves. When this happens, children are primarily mimicking the violent and militaristic content they've been exposed to and not working through the content in a way that builds their own political ideas and understandings. This is when children are most likely to be learning harmful lessons about violence.

Cause for Concern Using Both Lenses

Much of the play we hear about is children running around imitating the violent actions of characters they see on violent television programs or in films—like we described in several examples in Chapters 1 and 2. Given this state of affairs, we see cause for concern whichever lens we use to look at the war play of today.

From a developmental perspective, as children consume more media, they have less time to play. As they are exposed to increasing amounts of violence, especially on the screen, they have more violent content to bring to their play. But then, much of the play seems to be more imitative than creative. This kind of imitative play is not likely to be meeting children's needs. And, as children merely imitate violence rather than incorporate it into a rich play scenario of their own making, from a sociopolitical perspective they are more likely to learn negative lessons about violence.

From a sociopolitical perspective, when the quality of children's creative play is undermined and children are exposed to large amounts of violence, the concepts they form are more likely to mirror the violence they have seen and to be harmful. Furthermore, when war play is dominated by violent scripts that come from the media and by media-linked war toys that keep children focused on violence, it's hard for children to move on to more constructive play. In this situation, the violence they use may provide a sense of pseudo power at the moment it is used; but is not likely to help children develop the sense of inner power that can come from experiencing the deep sense of control and mastery that creative play can offer.

These disconnects between children's needs and behaviors can lead to many of the concerns adults report about current war play, such as aggressive and hard-to-manage play, children seemingly obsessed with war play, and children who bring the violence they use in their play to their everyday interactions and conflicts outside of the play. While many parents and teachers we talked with tended to criticize one another for causing the increased aggression and violence in children's play, this is generally misplaced blame.

We feel that a strong case can be made for concluding that changes in society, especially changes in the media and toy industries (which tend to reflect the broader political climate), are leading to many of the concerns about war play that currently are causing the war play dilemma to be felt with such intensity by so many adults.

CONCLUSION: WAR PLAY TODAY AND THE TWO VIEWS

We can now say that there are possible theoretical explanations for the concerns many adults currently are expressing about war play. From the developmental viewpoint, such play may not be serving children's needs to the degree that it once did. From the sociopolitical viewpoint, the play may be becoming more violent and militaristic. Each of these views has the potential for contributing to the understanding of the other: Parents and teachers cannot optimally affect the development of children's political ideas without considering the developmental perspective, and, if we address only developmental issues, we are not fully appreciating the political influences on children's lives today.

Where does this leave us in deciding how to respond to war play? We will need an approach for working with children that incorporates both the developmental and sociopolitical points of view, in order to address fully children's and adults' needs in these times.

4

Taking a Close Look at War Play Today

Paying close attention to children's play will help us learn to recognize the degree to which it is primarily creative play and coming from the children themselves or mainly imitative. Observing also can tell us a great deal about how children are using the play to work out developmental issues as well as the kinds of sociopolitical learning that might be occurring. The children in the three scenarios that follow are involved in play with violent themes. The content from each scenario is connected in some way to violence the children have seen.

JACKSON TAMES THE DINOSAURS

The subject in this scenario, Jackson, does not watch many violent cartoon programs or have the toys that accompany these programs. He engaged in the following play sequence after visiting a museum where he saw an animated movie in which a tyrannosaurus rex terrorized the other dinosaurs and then killed and ate a pterodactyl in a violent and bloody scene. That evening, playing at home, Jackson went and got out his own collection of dinosaurs. Here's what he did:

Jackson picks up his toy tyrannosaurus and crashes it into other dinosaurs, knocking them down and saying, "I'm smashing your bones. I got your eyes. I'm gonna grind you up . . . eat you up." He keeps hitting the dinosaurs with the tyrannosaurus over and over again with ferocity. Jackson hands a brontosaurus to his grandmother and tells her, "Say, 'Oh, please don't kill me. I don't wanna die' when the tyrannosaurus comes." The grandmother does this, but

Jackson's tyrannosaurus smashes her dinosaur to the ground as he says, "You're dead."

Jackson next picks up two dinosaurs and has one say to the other, "Quick, put your head in my mouth. I won't hurt you. I'm going to help you." The "helping" dinosaur carries the "victim" dinosaur in its mouth to a hiding place behind the couch as Jackson says, "Stay here. You're safe." One by one Jackson puts each of the dinosaurs' heads into the mouth of the "helper" and deposits them behind the couch. Then, this helping dinosaur goes and smashes into the tyrannosaurus, saying, "You're dead." Jackson grabs a stick from his toy drum set and hits the tyrannosaurus. "Now the other dinosaurs will be safe," he says. He carries the tyrannosaurus to another room and brings all the other dinosaurs out from behind the couch while singing, "Yeah, yeah, the tyrannosaurus is dead" (to the tune of "Ding, Dong, The Witch Is Dead" from *The Wizard of Oz*). Jackson says, "Now, the whole family is safe." He then goes to get the tyrannosaurus, saying, "You're going to have to live in a cage." He builds an elaborate cage for the tyrannosaurus and says, "He used to be in the family, but he's so bad they kicked him out."

Jackson's play grows out of his exposure to the violent cartoon and involves the themes of power and mastery, good and bad, and violence. As we look at this play scenario, we can see how it changes from beginning to end. In the beginning, Jackson uses only information he brings in from the cartoon; then he begins to take information he has learned from other experience and apply it to this situation (e.g., he incorporates his experience with his family and with a book he was read in which small animals hide in the mouth of a lion). It begins as repetitive violence with a single focus, becomes violence within a story context, and ends as violence overcome and restrained (i.e., tyrannosaurus in a cage). At first, the world is a threatening and hostile place; by the end it becomes a place where the family of dinosaurs can live in peace and safety. In addition, the play begins with Jackson taking the point of view and assuming the power of the mighty and scary tyrannosaurus. He gradually incorporates the point of view of the victim ("Oh, please don't kill me"). Finally, he stands back as the orchestrator of a "small world" of characters where power shifts to his family of "good" dinosaurs.

As we look at Jackson's play we can see that it seems to progress through a series of phases. In the first phase, Jackson primarily imitates what he has seen; he hits his toy dinosaurs with the tyrannosaurus rex over and over again. This is a fairly rigid phase in which he is using something new that he has experienced (the violent cartoon scene) in the form in which he has seen it. In the next phase, Jackson begins to elaborate the new idea, to introduce a variation on the cartoon script, by bringing in his grandmother and her role. Then he enters a third phase in which he really begins to invent a new story: He creates new roles (e.g., the helping dinosaur); uses new props (e.g., the couch, the other room); and brings his own concerns into the play, especially separation (feelings of being included in or excluded from the family) and mastery (overcoming fear from having seen the scary cartoon).

Jackson is feeling comfortable enough to experiment freely with major variations on the original idea. He is able to use the play to work on his own developmental concerns and to construct his own understanding of concepts. For example, he tries out one way of eliminating the threat of the tyrannosaurus (by killing it) and then experiments with another, less violent means (by building a cage). As he does this, Jackson's understanding of violence and how to resolve conflicts expands a little. He also learns about cooperation as he devises ways that the dinosaurs can help one another. This is the phase in which the active invention of new ideas occurs. It is the phase of play in which Jackson takes full control, making his own meaning out of a new experience. Toward the end of the play scenario, Jackson reaches a final phase in which he finds a resolution to the story; he creates a world free of the threat of tyrannosaurus rex and, along with this, experiences a sense of his own empowerment.

POW, POW, POWER RANGERS

Not long after having watched the television program, 4- and 6-year-old Mighty Morphin Power Ranger fans Anton and Phil are sitting together on an imaginary airplane using their collection of Power Ranger action figures. They repeatedly push a button on the backs of the figures that "morphs" (transforms) their faces from those of regular high schoolers to Power Rangers wearing masks and back again. Next, the boys take Power Rangers in each hand and begin bumping them against the chairs in front of them with accompanying "Pow, Pow" sounds. Soon, they begin to playfully karate chop each other with the figures. As the figures are put down and the boys get off the "plane," they begin using their own bodies to karate chop at each other, making the same "Pow, Pow" sounds. Suddenly, Anton launches a kick that actually hits Phil in the knee. As Phil bursts into tears and yells at Anton, Anton insists, "But it was just pretend, it wasn't real."

Anton and Phil are playing with Power Ranger action figures that are highly realistic replicas of the characters on the long-lasting, highly popular Mighty Morphin Power Ranger television show. They are focusing on those actions that the toys were designed to perform: kicking, karate chopping, and "morphing" back and forth between high schoolers with faces like the actors who play their parts on the television show and Power Ranger superheroes with masked faces. As this scenario changes, it stays focused primarily on the fighting aspects of the Power Rangers; the figures fight with each other, then hit objects around them, and when the figures are put away the boys use their bodies to karate chop each other. And as is often the case when children imitate violence, they end up with someone getting hurt, without having had any intention of doing so.

From a developmental perspective, since Anton and Phil are bringing to their play the karate-chopping action that they have seen the Power Rangers do on television, they seem to be trying to work out an understanding. The action figure toys, which are realistic replicas of the television characters, however, are used for one thing: pretend fighting. Similar to the previous scenario with Jackson, this play begins with the boys imitating the most graphic and dramatic aspects of the violence. Here, however, the play stays focused on the violence from the Power Ranger television show—the karate chops and fighting—with little other content. The only evolution in the play seems to be their increasingly hard karate chops. Little resolution of the story or violence is evident. As we observe the children's play, we learn little about what the violence means to them or what they are struggling to work out and understand. Compared with the earlier play scenario, Anton and Phil seem to be taking a less active role (even though they are physically active) and using less creativity, imagination, or skills to transform what they saw on television into something that is uniquely meaningful to them. The developmental lens leads us to question whether the boys' play is meeting their needs as fully as the play of the previous child. If not, then there is cause for concern because the play is not truly serving their developmental interests; it is *imitation*, not *creative play*.

Using a sociopolitical lens also leads to worrisome conclusions. Throughout their play, Phil and Anton focus on imitating the same violent actions of the Power Rangers over and over again. They do not seem to explore that violence, its effects on others, or alternatives to it. In this situation, it seems as if they are less likely than children who take charge and transform their play, to be learning the deeper lessons about violence and nonviolence that could counteract the glorification of the violence they see on the screen.

The contrast between Jackson's play and that of Anton and Phil is striking. If this play is representative of their play in general, then the implications for the overall development of each child can be significant. Jackson plays in a way that child development and play theory have long described as vital to healthy development. Anton and Phil play in a way that typifies many of the descriptions teachers and parents have given us as they express their concerns about how children's play at present is harmful to children and might be different than in the past.

NEWS VIOLENCE MAKES THE WALLS COME TUMBLIN' DOWN

For the fourth time in 20 minutes, 4-year-olds Wanda and Shelley have made a building with large hollow blocks. Wanda carefully crawls inside and Shelley starts to crash the building down with his fists and feet and yells, "Bang, Pow, Pow, Crash." As he continues kicking and shouting, Wanda, who is now buried under the blocks, yells, "Help me, I'm trapped. My house just blew up on me. I'm trapped. I can't move. Help, Help!" While the first 3 building demolitions ended with Wanda "dead" under the collapsed building, this time as she calls out for help, Shelley frantically starts pulling blocks off the pile and shouting, "Don't worry, here I come, here I come." Then he enthusiastically pulls a laughing Wanda out of the wreckage. Within minutes they begin rebuilding again.

Shelley and Wanda's play grows out of what they have heard about people getting buried soon after the Oklahoma City federal building was bombed. Their bringing such news to their play in this way is not unique. We heard many accounts of similar play in the months after the World Trade Center tragedy as well as after the tsunami tragedy in Asia.

Wanda and Shelley use their block play to re-enact the Oklahoma City bombing, including what happened to the people involved. They actually re-enact the same situation several times. But finally, they change what they do so that, by the end, instead of the scenario ending with Wanda "dead"—one consequence of violence—they finally have figured out a way to have a positive effect: rescuing the victim and making sure she is *safe.*

From a developmental perspective, while the teacher might wish that these children had not heard about the bombing or brought what they heard to the classroom, the intensity of their involvement and the details of their play suggest that they are working on something that is vitally important to them. It seems that once they heard about the bombing in Oklahoma City, their play became an important vehicle for working out their understanding, questions, and concerns; that it helped them reach some degree of resolution and gain a renewed sense of safety.

As Wanda and Shelley play, they focus on those aspects of what they heard that are most understandable at their level of development: the most graphic and concrete aspects of the situation, that is, the people getting buried in the building when it collapsed. They use what they already know—for instance, how it feels to be buried under a pile of blocks, what an explosion might be like, how a rescue operation works—as the starting point for working out their ideas. Their considerable skills in using blocks as a play material and in playing together contribute to their ability to use their play to work out the bombing in a meaningful way. Their play also provides adults with information about what the children have heard, how they understand what they have heard, and what else they may need in order to work through their concerns.

From a sociopolitical perspective, we need to ask what the children might be learning about violence and how people treat one another. The excitement of the early scenes seems to glorify and emphasize the violence as Shelley pretends to hurt Wanda while he knocks down the building. The play evolves so that Shelley also becomes the helper and rescuer. The children, therefore, are not left merely with a sense of the excitement that comes from the violence of knocking down a building, with no awareness of the consequences that violence can have. Nor are they merely experiencing the sense of helplessness and fear that violence often can instill. Instead, they are working through an understanding of the effects of violence on people and objects, while directly experiencing the empowering and reassuring message that people can and do help in ways they can understand through their own actions. By the end, Wanda and Shelley are learning positive social messages, for instance, about how to help hurt people, which are meaningful in their own immediate world. At the same time, they are neither asking the same questions nor working out the same understandings that adults would.

CONCLUSION

Using the developmental and sociopolitical lenses to look at these three play episodes points to the fact that there are fundamental differences in the nature and possible functions of play with violence. On the one hand, the play in the first and third scenarios shows children working on social, moral, and intellectual issues in positive ways, especially given that they were exposed to violence that they are trying to master. On the other hand, Anton and Phil's play points to potentially worrisome conclusions about the lessons they are learning about violence as fun and exciting. We also do not see them working out their needs and progressing to new, more advanced levels of understanding. So let's now explore where this newly focused lens leaves us in figuring out how to solve the war play dilemma in today's world.

PART III

STRATEGIES FOR RESOLVING THE WAR PLAY DILEMMA

5

To Ban or Not to Ban?
Is That the (Right) Question?
Deciding on an Approach to War Play

When we talk to parents and teachers about how they deal with war play in their homes and group settings, they often express ambivalence about what they are doing; few seem totally satisfied with whatever approach they are using. However, for the most part, their responses fall into one of the two sides of the war play debate—either they allow or they try to ban the play. But there is some variation in how they try to do this, and we find it helpful to group their responses into four approaches (listed below). We have added a fifth option for consideration:

Option 1: Ban war play
Option 2: Take a laissez-faire approach to war play
Option 3: Allow war play, with predetermined limits
Option 4: Actively facilitate war play
Option 5: Limit war play, but provide alternative ways to work on the issues

Most of the parents and teachers we questioned ban war play. They tend to see the play more in terms of its significance for political socialization and their role and responsibility in children's socialization. Some also ban it because they find that children often end up getting hurt or the play gets out of control.

There are also many adults who do allow war play in some form. They tend to see the play more in terms of its relationship to child development and their role and responsibility in supporting that development. It seems that, in choosing an approach to war play, adults often are making a choice, implicitly or explicitly, as to which of their roles and responsibilities with children they want to emphasize.

At the same time, no matter what approach they choose for responding to war play, many parents and teachers seem aware that they are not adequately addressing the other side of the debate—they are not addressing the war play dilemma.

Let's look more carefully at the various options in terms of how well they address the concerns of both the developmental and sociopolitical views. That is, how well does each nurture children's development and help them meet their needs? And, what lessons might children be learning in relation to violence and the social and political world?

OPTION 1: BAN WAR PLAY

> We have a strictly enforced "no guns in school" rule. If a child persists after the rule is explained ("guns hurt people—we don't even want to pretend to hurt people"), the child is put in time-out. . . . And unfortunately, some children seem to be obsessed with it and end up in time-out pretty often.

With the banning approach, adults tell children they are not allowed to engage in any kind of war and weapons play, sometimes giving an explanation and sometimes not. A lot of teachers and many parents choose this option because, in keeping with the sociopolitical view, they feel that allowing the play leads to the development of militaristic attitudes and hurtful behaviors. When they ban war play, they do not have to experience the discomfort that can arise when the play conflicts with their own desire to teach nonviolence. In fact, adults even feel that by banning the play they actually are teaching nonviolence, as they take a stand that violence, even when it's pretend, is bad. Finally, the banning approach is also attractive to adults because it eliminates the "discipline" problems and lack of a sense of safety that often result from war play.

But, based on the discussion in earlier chapters, we can now see that the banning option takes a powerful vehicle away from children that they could use to meet their developmental needs. If children need violent play to work out an understanding of the war-related images and content they are exposed to, then adults who ban it are depriving children of that option. At a time when children are exposed to a lot of violence in their daily lives and can have an increased need to work through that violence through play, we need to consider the impact banning might have on them.

From a developmental view, banning war play can lead to additional problems. When adults tell children that war play is "wrong" or "bad" (e.g., "guns hurt people—we don't even want to pretend to hurt people"), we run the risk of making children feel guilty or bad about themselves for trying to meet their needs. Even gently telling children they can't engage in war play at home or school can create problems. It conveys the message that they can't turn to adults for help in working out something that fascinates, confuses, or even worries them. And as adults we lose one important channel for reaching out to children to help them meet their needs.

From a sociopolitical perspective, banning war play can result in children hiding the things that really interest or concern them from the important adults in their lives, and perhaps learning harmful lessons about violence. It leaves children to their own devices to work out an understanding of the violence they have seen. And especially worrisome, it prevents us from having any direct influence on what children are learning about violence and social behavior as they engage in war play outside of their teachers' or parents' view. By choosing not to influence the political concepts that children are constructing in their play, we are, in effect, giving up one central avenue we have for affecting what children learn from the violence they see.

In sum, while the banning approach helps adults feel that they are teaching children nonviolence, it does not adequately take into account our responsibility to children. It can seem to eliminate problems and controversy from the home and classroom, but it leaves too much of children's development—the meeting of their needs and the growth of their political understanding—to social forces outside of the classroom and home.

OPTION 2: TAKE A LAISSEZ-FAIRE APPROACH TO WAR PLAY

> The kids in my classroom love war play. I think they need to be able to play in their own way without my interference, so I don't usually get involved unless someone is getting hurt.

With the laissez-faire approach in its pure form, adults openly allow children to play in whatever ways they choose, including war play. In its more diluted form, perhaps because of ambivalence about war play, we turn our backs and allow the play, without directly condoning it. This option appeals to many who basically want to support children's needs and who see that children have a genuine interest in war play. It can be a positive thing for children to feel that the parent or teacher accepts their needs and the forms of play that they enjoy.

How does the laissez-faire approach hold up through our two lenses? It does create the potential for children to work on their developmental needs through war play. But, when we put the whole burden of working it out on children themselves, we are leaving to chance whether their needs are met. In other kinds of dramatic play, such as house play, adults often take on a more active role as facilitators (such as by suggesting a new role or prop). When we use a laissez-faire approach, we are leaving children to develop the play themselves to the extent that they can do it on their own. By choosing not to get involved in or influence war play, we are relinquishing an area in which we could have an impact.

In addition, our nonparticipation leaves the question of *safety* up to the children. The violent content of the war play, and how they enact it, can make children feel unsafe. This can affect the quality of the play and the extent to which children are able to use their play to work on key issues. Children vary considerably in their ability to keep their play safe for themselves. It is rarely the case that all children will be able to feel secure in war play if an adult is not providing any external controls. And we often hear how war play today gets out of control and feels unsafe.

Can the laissez-faire approach fulfill the adult's responsibility in influencing the lessons children learn from their war play? As with the banning approach, when we are not involved in the play, children are left to their own imitation of the violent images they have seen. We leave children with their own ideas—often rigid and stereotypical ones—about the violence, without helping them.

In sum, the laissez-faire option does not adequately address the concerns of either the developmental or sociopolitical views. At a time when the quality of children's creative play is being called into question, and when children seem to need help in developing their war play and the political concepts it involves, it seems doubtful adopting the laissez-faire approach is the best choice.

OPTION 3: ALLOW WAR PLAY, WITH SPECIFIED LIMITS

I allow the play to go on outside as long as no one gets hurt. The rule is usually that it's okay outdoors if all parties are willing participants and if it's done with pretend, not toy, guns.

This is a variation on the laissez-faire approach. Here adults allow the play, but they place clearly spelled-out limits on it. They may specify where the play can occur, such as only in the playground or backyard or in the block area or basement. They may place limits on the times when the play can occur, such as only at the beginning of the day or at recess. Limits may be placed on the materials allowed for the play, such as no toy weapons, only fingers; only child-made weapons such as cardboard tubes; no action figures. There also may be rules that guide the social interactions in the play; for example, children must all agree to engage in the play or agree on what roles they will assume or refrain from actual physical contact.

This option can be attractive to adults because, as with the laissez-faire approach, children do have the opportunity to use war play to meet their needs. Because of the clearly spelled-out limits, it is more likely than the laissez-faire approach to help children stay in control and feel safe as they play. Adults also can be more in control of what happens because they are creating some boundaries for the play, often even stating clear limits on the degree of violence that occurs. In a sense, this is a *middle-of-the-road* approach that begins to address both developmental and sociopolitical issues.

But there are limits as to how well this approach addresses the concerns of both lenses. In terms of developmental issues, with this approach, as with the laissez-faire approach, little attention is given to the adult's role in facilitating the play process. Therefore, while the play is allowed, the degree to which children succeed in meeting their developmental needs is still left up to them.

In terms of the sociopolitical lens, if an adult limits the play in certain ways but does not become actively involved in working with it, then the political and social concepts that a child is working out are, once again, left to the child and other societal forces. There is little meaningful connection between the ideas children are working out in their play and adult values and goals. Because toy guns are not allowed in their war play, children may know that a parent or teacher disapproves of guns, but how does this fit with the many things they have heard about guns, war, and politics outside the home and classroom—things that have become part of their play?

We feel that this approach is less than ideal because it restricts the adult role in terms of both facilitating the play and influencing the ideas children learn.

OPTION 4: ACTIVELY FACILITATE WAR PLAY

It has taken me a long time to accept children's need to engage in war play in my classroom. I've had to get past a lot of obstacles in my own thinking. But this year I have been allowing the play with some limits. And I've become involved in the play myself, observing children and intervening in a lot of different ways.

This teacher has decided to allow war and weapons play and take a constructive role in facilitating it. Parents have described attempting a similar approach, commonly after one of the other approaches hasn't worked.

Using this approach involves trying to figure out how children are using their play to work out feelings and ideas. While not taking control of the play away from children, we can help them expand and elaborate their play—suggesting new roles, offering new materials, temporarily assuming a role in the play. We also can have conversations with children about the play and its content, when they are not playing. Such efforts can help children expand their play beyond the narrow focus on imitating violence. Our facilitation also can foster creativity and problem-solving ability during play.

This approach is difficult for many of us to accept. It asks us to get involved in something many of us would prefer to banish permanently from children's lives. It places extra demands on us to pay closer attention to the play than many of us would choose to do. We end up bearing the burden of trying to influence what happens in the play and what children learn, while at the same time trying to keep the play safe.

Despite the discomfort we may feel, there are two central reasons why this option can be the most effective approach for dealing with the war play dilemma of today. First, when children are allowed to engage in war play in which we take an active role, it provides an opportunity for them to work on several key issues. It can help them:

- Engage in creative play versus imitation
- Gain control over their aggressive impulses
- Take a point of view other than their own
- Distinguish between fantasy and reality
- Work out an understanding of what they have heard about the world around them
- Experience a sense of their own power and mastery through play

The second major reason for adopting this approach is that, both in and out of their play, it increases our influence over the political and moral ideas children develop. That is, the concepts that children bring to their play—about the nature of enemies and friends, good and bad, war and peace, and violence as a means of solving conflicts with others—

come within the realm of our influence. We can attempt to influence these concepts at the children's level of development and interest and, by so doing, act as positive agents of political socialization.

For these two reasons, we feel that Option 4 is often the strongest one available to us for resolving the war play dilemma. As we'll see in Chapter 6, what is involved in implementing it will vary from child to child, home to home, and classroom to classroom. This is because we need to follow the lead from children themselves for what to do.[1]

There will be settings where war play will not be a big issue and we will not need to do a lot to implement this option. However, even in such a situation we will need to consider what children are being exposed to when they are not with us and how we want to become involved in influencing what they learn from it. For those adults who decide to implement Option 4 more fully, it is a complex and difficult approach. It places yet another demand on us as parents and teachers. It asks us to take on responsibility for helping children with yet another "problem" created by the society at large. And, there will be instances when, even with the best efforts of adults, Option 4 can not be safely implemented. For these situations we have added Option 5.

OPTION 5: LIMIT WAR PLAY, BUT PROVIDE ALTERNATIVE WAYS TO WORK ON THE ISSUES

I've been trying to let war play happen. I've even managed to give some good ideas that have helped improve the quality of the play. We've had some good conversations about "pretend" fighting too. But no matter what I do to keep the violence from getting out of hand, it feels like the minute I turn my back, someone gets hurt or someone seems scared. No matter what I've tried, I haven't found a way to keep things safe. I know it's what some kids like to do best—are even obsessed about, but I've had to put a stop to the play.

Some adults, especially teachers, who have attempted to work with war play, as suggested in Option 4, tell us too many problems still occur with the play. They also say that they have one or more children who are so obsessed with war play that it seems to be on their minds all the time and the violent content is brought into most things they do. This seems to be especially true with children who spend a lot of time consuming media, especially violent media.

With Option 5, we limit war play but help children work on war play-related issues in other ways. That is, we find ways to help children work on war play themes through alternative activities such as art and drawing, building, conversations, and using children's books. While these same activities often are used in conjunction with Option 4, in this case they take on more importance.

Option 5 has become more appealing to many teachers and some parents because they see the dramatic effects on certain children of the cross-marketing of violent themes through TV shows, video games, movies, toys, books, and other products. As we have pointed out, this saturation through media floods some children's minds and results in imitative and repetitious play that seems obsessive and hard to modify. The marketing influence is so compelling for some children that they do not seem to be able to get these themes off their minds or use them to play in ways that meet their needs. In these cases, adults can encourage children to express their interests in alternative ways. Drawing, writing, building, reading, and talking are avenues of expression that use symbols that provide more distance than does dramatic play, which engages the whole child in acting out a role. When a child builds a house for Spider-Man, for example, he maintains a separation from the character; but when the child acts out the role of Spider-Man, he "becomes" this character—he can have a harder time staying separate and letting his own ideas shape what happens.

With our encouragement, children can use these alternative avenues of expression to work on war play-related themes in ways that will help them bring their own creativity and ideas into the process. We can encourage the use of open-ended materials and the incorporation of children's ideas so as not to reproduce replicas of media characters and events. This will help children continue to build their own ideas and make their own meaning out of any violence they have seen.

When we implement Option 5, we can tell children that we are banning war play because children are getting hurt, or it's too scary, even though everyone has tried to keep it safe. At the same time we can suggest what they can do, such as have a special time when they can make pictures and dictate stories about the characters and themes they like. We also can have special times when we have conversations with them about the war play they do in other places—so they know that we are interested in it and willing to talk to them about their play.

We feel that this approach—when adults make a real commitment to helping children use alternative activities—can meet the key criteria spelled out for resolving the war play dilemma. It provides children with avenues for working on their developmental needs (such as the violence they've seen). It also ensures we will engage with them around the content they are trying to figure out and the lessons they learn.

In the chart below we provide an overview of the five options for addressing the war play dilemma.

**Summary and Evaluation of the Five Options
for Resolving the War Play Dilemma**

Options for solving the war play dilemma	Can it meet developmental needs?	Can it address sociopolitical learning?
1. Ban all war play	No	Maybe
2. Take a laissez-faire approach	Maybe	No
3. Allow war play, with limits	Maybe	No
4. Actively facilitate war play	Yes	Yes
5. Limit war play but provide alternative ways to work on the issues	Yes	Yes

PARENTS AND TEACHERS:
WORKING TOGETHER (AND APART)

While many parents and teachers say they started out trying to ban war play, many more parents than teachers say they eventually ended up allowing the play in some form (choosing Option 2 or 3). This happened because they could see that their children wanted and seemed to need to play this way. While we do not have a large enough sample to draw any definitive conclusions, it is interesting to speculate about what might account for this apparent difference between teachers' and parents' choices.

Unique Aspects of Parents' and Teachers' Roles

The different roles that parents and teachers have with respect to children and society and the different constraints on their interactions with children may help account for the differences we found. Parents are responsible for individual children and can base their responses on the particular needs of their child, whom they know very well. As they watch and identify particular interests and needs, they can modify their attitudes and responses. Teachers, on the other hand, are responsible for groups of children and also to society. They often base their responses on the more "universal" needs and interests of groups. They also cannot focus on individual children's responses and needs to the extent that parents do. Teachers generally view the needs of the individual in the context of the group and are less likely to sacrifice the needs of the group for the needs of individuals.

In dealing with war play by responding to the needs and interests of their individual children, parents are coming down more on the developmental side of the war play debate. Teachers, on the other hand, are more likely to develop rules and policies that address their responsibilities to the whole group and society, coming down on the sociopolitical side of the debate.

Despite the different situations of parents and teachers, we still feel that, to the extent possible, Option 4 is the best approach for resolving the war play dilemma for both groups. It optimizes the opportunities for children to have both their developmental and sociopolitical needs met at home and at school. And even better, the more parents and teachers can work together and support each other's efforts, the better the solutions are likely to be.

Beyond Blame

One obstacle we have found that can stand in the way of parents and teachers working together is that they sometimes blame each other for the problems they are having with their children's war play. Teachers often blame parents for letting their children see violence on the screen or have war toys. They reason that children would not convey such a strong need to bring war play to the group setting if parents played a more active role in protecting children. And parents, who work hard to protect their children from exposure to war play, war toys, and violent media, say that their children are exposed to such content at school and teachers are to blame.

We feel that this blame usually is misplaced. No one can protect children from all the violence that permeates society, including childhood culture. Some of it will get in no matter what we do, and when it does, children will try to work it out in their play. So the best solution is to work together and support each other's efforts to help children.

In Chapter 6, let us look more closely at what is involved in putting Options 4 and 5 into practice in ways that will help resolve the war play dilemma.

6

Guidelines for Resolving the War Play Dilemma

There are many practical strategies that can help us become more effective at dealing with children's war play. They are connected to almost every level at which we work and interact with children, far beyond just dealing with the play itself. Many of them will grow out of things we already do. Others may require shifting to new ways of thinking and being with children.

GUIDELINE 1

Limit children's exposure to violence, including violent media and products linked to it, as much as possible.

Our efforts to deal with the war play dilemma need to begin by addressing one of the most powerful forces contributing to the problem—the massive exposure children have in our society to violence in the media and the popular culture. The more we can protect children from this violence, the less need they will have to engage in war play and the less we will have to struggle to deal with it. And while we can't fully protect them, there *is* a lot we can do to make things better than they currently are. And the better we get at it, the more everyone—except those who make money from marketing violence to children—will benefit.

Strategies

- *Learn about the TV programs and other media in children's lives (as well as the popular products linked to them).* When you are familiar with the shows, videos, films, and computer games, then you will be in a better position to work with children about what is and is not okay to watch, as well as engage in conversations about the shows with children who see them.

- *Teach children how to make good choices about the media they watch.* This is a gradual process. Advance planning is key to making good viewing choices. The younger the child, the more the adult should be in control of what is seen. Then, offering a choice between two shows, and then three, and talking about reasons for making choices, can help children themselves learn how to become thoughtful consumers of media. By kindergarten or first grade, children can keep viewing logs to plan what they will watch.

- *Work out routines as to when media are and are not consumed.* Remember that media are very seductive and often lure children into wanting more and more, thereby gradually squeezing out other more child-controlled activities. Having definite times of the day when children watch (before dinner for half an hour) and times when they don't (for instance, for an hour before bedtime) can help avoid the constant hassles and nags about when it is and when it is not okay to watch. Having routines around interesting things children do when they are not watching (for instance, helping to set the table before dinner can provide a sense of competence and being a part of the family) also can help to avoid struggles.

- *When children are exposed to media involving violence, help them deal with what they have seen.* Talk to children openly about it and listen carefully to what they say. Such conversations can occur both at home and at school. Some examples of questions to use in conversations with children about violent content are provided in the chart on the following page.

- *Work with other parents and professionals to support one another's efforts to protect children from media violence and counteract its negative impact.* The more we create communities that support mutual efforts, the more powerful we can become in protecting children from the onslaught. Schools can do a great deal to support parents in their efforts to deal with media violence in children's lives. Having parents meet to discuss how to manage media violence and the violence marketed to children through the media (and why it's important to do so) can help to create such a community. Such an effort can provide a climate where professionals talk to children about the media in their lives and help children learn to manage and deal with media violence. It also can create a climate where it is easier for parents to talk together and support one another's efforts to limit the influence of media culture on their children.

Questions to Guide Conversations About Media Violence

- Discuss each other's reactions (both positive and negative) to what you saw:
  What did you think about that show/game?
  Did you like it when _____ happened? Why do you think it
  happened?
  I didn't like it when _____. I wish they didn't have to hurt each other.
  What do you think?

- Help children sort out fantasy from reality:
  What was pretend and what was real? How could you tell?

- Help clarify confusion by saying things such as, "In real life things don't work
  that way." "I wonder how they made _____ happen on that show."

- Help children develop an understanding of advertisements and advertising:
  How can we tell the difference between these ads and the show?
  I wonder why they made that toy look so exciting? Do you think it can
  really do that?

- Compare what children see on the program to their own experience:
  Could anything like _____ happen to you? When? How could it be the
  same/different?
  What would you do if you were in that situation?

- Talk about the violence and other mean-spirited behavior that children see on
  the screen:
  What do you think about how _____ solved their problem?
  If you had a problem like that, what could you do/say?
  Can you think of a way to solve that problem where no one gets hurt?

- Ask questions that focus on stereotyped images and behaviors:
  I wonder why it's always men with big muscles that go to fight? Did you
  notice that?
  The women always seem to need to get rescued by men. Have you noticed
  that? I wonder why?
  I wonder why the "bad guys" have foreign accents? Wear dark colors? Have
  darker skin?

Adapted from: *Remote Control Childhood: Combating the Hazards of Media Culture* by Diane
Levin (Washington, DC: National Association for the Education of Young Children, 1998),
p. 139.

GUIDELINE 2

Help children learn to engage in creative and meaningful dramatic play of all kinds.

With the large amount of screen time, highly structured media-linked and electronic toys, and pressures to focus on basic skills rather than play, it can be a big challenge to ensure that children become involved in creative and meaningful dramatic play. Many children no longer fully develop this essential ability in their everyday lives. Yet, the better able they are to engage in this kind of play, the better equipped they will be to create war play that meets their needs, as addressed by the developmental side of the war play debate.

The space, time, and materials you provide all can contribute to the quality of children's play. Whatever your resources (often less is better than more), you can support children's play through careful intervention and facilitation and by creating an environment that shows you support and value their play.

Strategies

- *Find times and places where children can play without frequent interruptions.* One reason children don't learn how to get deeply involved in play is that they are used to getting interrupted. If every time they start to take off with their play, something interferes—for instance, another children grabs a toy, a television is turned on, or an adult asks them to move their playthings to a new place to "make room for dinner or snack time"—they quickly learn that it doesn't pay to get involved and invested in play.

  Building *regular playtimes* into children's daily routine helps them get used to playing without interruptions.

  Children should have a *special place* where they know they can play without disruptions. It need not be available at all times—just during playtime. Perhaps every day after lunch you create a special enclosure by putting a sheet over the table (or use a large appliance carton) and allow children to play under it—making a spaceship or a pirate's cave or a camping tent. If you see children starting to set up play in an inconvenient place, suggest an alternative location before they get too far.

  It is important to give a warning a few minutes before it's time for the play to stop, and to find ways to *preserve what children are working on* until the next playtime. This can help children sustain and deepen their play over time and learn that you value it.

- *Help children become familiar with the play materials that are available and where to find them.*

  An effective way to help children's play develop is to provide a *supply of interesting props* they are familiar with and can find readily. It's so easy for children to get distracted from play while going to search for a desired item.
  Children can be involved in *organizing and storing play materials*. Help them decide where to keep things. It can be hard for young children to organize objects into clear categories—for instance, categories for animal play, space play, and house play. Follow the children's lead for how to organize things, and use clean-up time as an opportunity to help them learn and review where things are kept. Then they will be able to find materials with less disruption to their play.
  Labeling toy storage bins with pictures that children can "read" also can help them find and clean up materials.

- *Look for opportunities to facilitate the play.* Play belongs to children. They should be the directors, scriptwriters, actors, and prop people. Ideally, adults shouldn't intervene too much. But there is variation in the amount of help children will need. Today, there are many children who have not become very capable creative players, engaging instead primarily in imitative play. These are the children who will need the most help developing and elaborating their play, although all children's play can benefit from help that doesn't take over or judge it. There are many techniques to try out both during and after the play.

  Making an occasional comment about what you see happening in the play is one technique. The comments can be brief and do not need to interrupt the flow: "I see the baby stopped crying when you gave her a bottle," or "You made that towel into a perfect cape." Comments like this show children that you appreciate what's happening in their play. Sometimes it can lead to further conversation or to elaboration of the play.
  Asking an open-ended question that has many possible answers is another powerful technique. Such questions let you provide input without being bossy. They can lead children to some new idea they might not have thought of themselves. For example, you might ask, "What

other things can the baby eat?" or "I wonder what else you could use that paper towel tube for?" There are no perfect questions, and what seems to work well one time might not work the next.

Providing an interesting play material at the right moment also can lead children in new directions. There is rarely one "right" item to introduce. Things work best that children can connect to and incorporate into what they already are doing. Often a simple item works best, like paper towel tubes, or cardboard boxes, or shiny scarves.

You also can help children *bring new content into their play.* Often the content that works best is something they have experienced directly themselves in some meaningful or exciting way. Having a birthday party, visiting a relative, getting a pet, going to the doctor, or learning to help set the table for dinner all can provide rich content we can help children bring to their play. More traumatic experiences like injuries, stays in the hospital, a fire in the neighborhood, getting lost in the supermarket, or breaking a favorite object are also potentially rich play themes.

When children have been playing a particular theme for a long time without a lot of variation, you can *help them get their play "unstuck."* Many children have favorite topics and roles that they play over and over again. As they do, their play usually will evolve and change as they master what they're working on, come up with new ways to play out old themes, and have new experiences to bring to the play. But when this does not seem to happen, actively introducing new content, such as a new character or a new action for existing characters, can help children find new problems and issues to work into their play.

GUIDELINE 3

When children engage in war play, learn as much as you can about the nature of the play and the issues they are working on.

A first step in working with children around their war and weapons play is to learn as much as you can about what individual children are expressing about their needs, developmental issues, political concepts, and concerns. This is important because it will serve as an essential guide for deciding how to work with the play and influence what children learn from it.

Strategies

- *Watch the children as they play to learn more about such issues as the following:*

  The themes and characters that are most important and what they mean to children.

  Where children get the ideas for the characters and "scripts" for the play—is it from direct experience, television programs or films, books, or their imagination?

  The nature of favorite toys and play materials; how structured they are (i.e., highly structured or of the children's own invention; media-linked, narrowly focused on fighting and violence); and how children use them.

  The degree to which children are imitating and repeating a particular script over and over or to which they are involved in creative play that they control and that evolves over time.

  The amount of time children spend involved in war play in relation to other forms of dramatic play they do, as well as in relation to other activities and interests.

  The degree to which the content of war play focuses narrowly on violence to the exclusion of other issues and carries over into the children's behavior outside of play.

  The developmental issues children are working on in their play (e.g., control and power, separation and autonomy, fantasy and reality, gender identification).

  The political ideas children are using in their play, such as the nature of friends and enemies, of conflict resolution, of death and killing.

  The areas in the play of individual children as well as groups that are likely to require adult guidance and support to maintain the emotional and physical safety of individual children and the group.

- *Talk to children about their play.* That way you can learn more about what the play means to them, what aspects trouble or confuse them most, and how they're able to distinguish between fantasy and reality.

GUIDELINE 4

In children's war play, address the issues raised by both the developmental and sociopolitical sides of the war play dilemma.

Many of the suggestions here parallel suggestions in Guideline 2 regarding helping children become good dramatic players. But, it's even more important for us to take an active role in influencing war play than other forms of play, because so much of the content of war play is highly imitative and narrowly focused on violence, and because so much of the process is repetitive and driven by media and not by children. But remember, there is a fine line between facilitating and intruding; we need to continually assess the impact of our interventions on children and their play. As we saw in the discussion of Guideline 2, we need to work to ensure that our efforts to facilitate play do not take control of the play away from the children.

Strategies

- *Know the "scene" in the popular culture that is influencing children's war play.* Even though it can be hard, it can be very helpful to keep track of the rapidly changing, most popular violent television programs, films, and toys that permeate the childhood culture at any given time. Without keeping up, it can be difficult to figure out what is going on in children's play and the factors that are influencing it, much less how to enter into it. Even when adults try to protect children from being exposed to current pop crazes or items, in many cases children still will be learning about them at school, on playgrounds, or from seeing images on products at stores.

- *Base interventions on the developmental issues children are working on in their play.* For instance, if a child tends to be confusing the fantasy of the play with reality, you should be there to clarify the boundary. A teacher might say, "Remember, Miles, Raun is only pretending to be the bad guy; he isn't really bad."

- *Base interventions on the cognitive understanding children reveal as they play* (as outlined in Chapter 2). For instance, if children don't make obvious connections between their actions and the effects they have, you can point out the consequences of their behavior: "If you jump from that platform, you'll hurt yourself. Remember what happened yesterday when you tried it."

- *Foster early political ideas in ways that build the concepts revealed in the play in less militaristic, more humanistic directions.* For example, if a group of children always portray the "bad guy" as attacking them, the teacher might try to expand their concept of the enemy: "Where does that bad guy go when he's not fighting with you?"

- *Bring new content into the war play that helps expand the play from a narrow focus on violence and fighting.* You can introduce new props, roles, and physical settings that grow out of the current content and serve to help children vary and elaborate their play. This is especially important for those children who seem to be closely following a "good guy"/"bad guy" television script or acting out the same violent theme over and over in the same way.

For example, if children are repeating one play scenario the same way day after day, you might try to change a feature of the setting by saying, "Today, the appliance carton [which has been a *Star Wars* spaceship for a long time] is going to be a ship in the Atlantic Ocean." You also could take the children to a new setting, such as a park, to encourage them to adapt their spaceship play to the new environment. The children's books listed in Appendix C also can provide compelling content.

- *Help the children who are good creative players maintain this quality in their play.* It is so easy to be swept up into the immediate excitement and power of the imitative war play of other children, that even the most capable players sometimes will need your support in keeping the play creative. In addition, with your help, these children's ideas and actions can help spur creative play for more imitative players.

  For instance, if a group of children is pretending that "The Hulk" is chasing them, the teacher can ask the one child with a personally invented monster who has magical powers, "Does your monster have a special power that can help protect the 'good guys' from 'The Hulk'?"

- *Make comments to accompany the play that relate to what the children are doing.* You might say, "I see the bad guys again; I wonder where they go." Or you could say, "You found a new way to travel through space today." Such comments do not necessarily intrude if the child does not want to be interrupted or channeled in a new direction. At the same time, they often elicit a commentary from the child about what she is doing. As a result the teacher may gain further insight into the child's play and get ideas about possible ways to help her elaborate it, and the child may even develop a plan for elaborating the play on her own, just by talking about what she is doing.

- *Talk about the themes in ways that have meaning for the children and try to avoid placing adult value judgments on the play.* This can help keep the communication going as well as facilitate the play. For instance, if a child is making a magic potion to "kill the bad guy," instead of saying, "You shouldn't kill," or "I don't like killing," say something like, "Wow, that stuff looks really powerful! What's going into the potion? What else can it do beside killing the bad guys?"

- *Use open-ended questions and comments related to the violent content in the play to help children find new problems to solve and to get beyond the narrow focus on violence.* Examples of such open-ended questions are: "I wonder if there's a way to capture the bad guy without killing him." "What can the bad guy do now that he's trapped?" "What can you do to get the bad guy to listen to you?" These can grow out of what is happening at any given moment and allow for many different responses, depending on the individual meaning the child makes of the question. They also open up new possibilities for children's play.

GUIDELINE 5

Work to counteract the lessons about violence and stereotyping that children may be learning in their war play.

Often, when children are actually involved in war play, they do not want to be interrupted and even resist our efforts to intervene. Sometimes we can have a bigger impact if we work on war play issues when the children are not actually playing. But whether in- or outside of the play, the goal is to help children expand their narrowly focused ideas and provide them with input that later will help to enrich the quality of their play and thinking.

Strategies

- *Give children opportunities to talk about the violence they bring into their play.* This is true of both pretend (entertainment) and real (news) violence. Adults often find it hard to talk about such violence with children, especially in a way that allows room for children to feel it's okay for them to say what they really think and know. And children often pick up on the fact that adults don't like to talk about this topic with them. We can ask children to tell us more about the characters they like and about their weapons and what they do. We can find many creative ways to open doors for conversations about war play and violence.
- *Try to expand and complicate children's thinking about the violent content of their war play.* As we saw in Chapter 2, children do not just take in and learn what we tell them they should about violence. Their ideas develop gradually over time. One way we can help their ideas develop is to try to complicate their thinking—that is, provide information that builds just a little bit onto what they already know, or that throws something they already know into question.

Children may need help to *sort out what is pretend and what is real.* Make comments such as, "I'm glad in real life things like that don't happen," or "On TV they made it look like you could jump out of a window onto a bad guy, but in real life people can't do that! They would get reallllllly hurt!"

You can try to *humanize the enemy* (e.g., "Oh dear, the bad guy's hurt. Can we find him a doctor?" or "I wonder what makes the bad guy need to fight so much. What do you think he does at night when he's finished fighting?").

You can help children understand the actual effects of aggression and violence (e.g., "I'm glad to see you and Miguel are just pretending to hit, because if you really hit each other you'll both get hurt"). Such comments illustrate how adults can bring information about violence to young children as they play, at the concrete and immediate level that they can understand, without making children feel bad or guilty.

- Help children bring the content of their war play into other kinds of activities. We can help children find and develop new interests and new ways of representing the war play content that excites them at the moment by bringing the play into the block area, the sand and water tables, and the writing and art areas. At home they might bring some of their plastic war play toys into the bathtub.

  These efforts can divert children's interests away from the narrow focus on violence and teach them other ways to meet their needs more removed from war play itself. They also can help children develop new skills and new interests, and deepen and extend the repertoire of actions and ideas they can bring to their war play.

  For example, if children in a classroom are using sticks as pretend walkie-talkies, the teacher could set up materials at the workbench and help the children build their own walkie-talkies. As the children work, the teacher could help them think about what characteristics the walkie-talkie needs to have, what materials are needed and how they can be used, and how this new instrument can be taken back into play. In addition to helping expand the children's concept of walkie-talkie and its use in the play, this activity also can lead to a new interest in woodworking, a growing sense of mastery with materials, and a curriculum unit around the theme of walkie-talkies.

- *Develop other curriculum activities and themes that satisfy the same developmental needs met by war play.* We can provide powerful alternative images to those offered by television and toys, but that still address such issues as mastery, power, and control and fit with the way young children view the world. There is a rich tradition of folklore and literature for young children and many possibilities for incorporating these into the curriculum. Children may need help elaborating the less concrete and salient images that come from nonelectronic media sources such as books, in order to use them meaningfully in their play.

One kindergarten teacher told us what she did when her classroom was dominated by repetitive and aggressive *Star Wars* play. She began reading the story of *The Wizard of Oz* at group time. She filled the dramatic play area of the classroom with props relating to the story. In class discussions of the story, she placed special emphasis on the issues that related to the concerns she felt children were expressing in their *Star Wars* play (e.g., power, control, and autonomy). She told us how the children gradually became immersed in playing out, drawing, and making props for the story of *The Wizard of Oz,* while at the same time the *Star Wars* play gradually diminished. (See Appendix B, "Two Sample Curriculum Webs.")

In addition to using books and stories, teachers can develop curriculum units on such themes as scary things, monsters, dinosaurs, and creatures from outer space. (See Appendix B, Web 2.) Such topics also lend themselves to many of the same developmental needs and interests children express in their war play.

- *Use the disputes that occur in war play as an opportunity to foster an understanding of conflict resolution.* The disagreements and conflicts that often arise in war play can become an opportunity to teach children about ways of dealing with conflicts that do not involve violence. What children learn from these efforts can counteract the lessons embedded in war play. They also can help children learn how to sustain their play instead of ending it every time a conflict occurs.

  Because conflicts in war play come from the children's firsthand experiences, they provide ideal, age-appropriate material for reflection and learning. Working through conflicts can help children learn about predicting and understanding the consequences of their actions, taking points of view other than their own, and considering more than one solution to a problem—all skills that make the use of violence to solve conflicts less necessary.

  In classrooms, teachers also can bring up actual conflicts that occurred in the play for everyone to discuss at class meetings. This is especially useful for ongoing issues or if several children have had similar problems. Chapter 7 presents an example of a teacher having a group discussion to work out an ongoing problem with Power Rangers play in the classroom.

GUIDELINE 6

Make keeping the play safe your highest priority.

Children learn and grow best in settings where they feel safe and in control.[1] When children do not trust that they are safe, a lot of their energy can go into trying to protect themselves and even into trying to be strong and powerful—as in war play and dealing with conflicts by fighting.

Even in settings where children do feel safe, war, weapons, and superhero play often can become scary and unpredictable for some children. Especially for children who have issues around feeling safe or who are working on impulse control in their play, there is the constant risk of losing control. For those children who are less involved in war play or are more in control, there can be the threat of being "shot at" or actually "attacked" by other children. Both groups of children need to trust that we can protect them and keep them safe from the loss of their own or others' control. Therefore, we need to think through how we can work with children in an ongoing way to create a safe context in which war play can occur.

Strategies

- *At school and at home, help every child experience a deep sense that "I AM SAFE HERE—my body is safe; my feelings are safe; my thoughts, ideas, and words are safe; and the things I make and do (including my war play) are safe."* This is the "Safety Rule."[2] It applies to everything we do with children and they do with one another, and it can be the basis for working out all sorts of situations with children. For instance, when children get into a conflict during war play, rather than getting angry or blaming them, we can use the "Safety Rule" by telling them, "Everyone grabbing for Tinkertoys to make swords doesn't feel safe. We all agreed that you could use the large Tinkertoys as a pretend sword, but Eli got hit. We have to find a way for you to do it that's safe for everyone. What can we do?"
- *When war play enters home or school, decide on the few basic limits that will help keep the play safe.* As children gain experience with these limits

and the need for new limits arises, they will be able to discuss and modify the limits with more concrete understanding of the possible implications.

- *When intervention is needed for safety's sake, try to enter into the war play in ways that do not stop it.* Help children work out solutions that give them a safe alternative for continuing their play. For instance, when play is deteriorating because two children both want the "fantasy cape," rather than saying, "You need to share or stop playing," the teacher can say, "I know how you can share it! I have an hour glass, and I'll show you how to use it to take turns."

- *When limits are needed, try not to place adult value judgments on the children's war play; rather, try to use the "Safety Rule."* For example, when a child hits another child, rather than saying, "It's bad to hit; stop it right now," you might say, "Even if Howie is pretending to be the 'bad guy,' when you hit him he gets hurt and that's not safe. I can't let you do that." Such an adult response helps children learn about the logical causal effects of their actions on others, rather than feel guilty or bad about themselves and not learn much about how to avoid the problem next time.

- *When the only way to ensure children's sense of safety is to stop the play, then the adult must do so.* This gets us to the issues outlined in Option 5 for dealing with war play. If this becomes necessary, we again can rely on the "Safety Rule" by saying, "We've really tried hard to find a way to play Power Rangers where everyone is safe. But it's not working. It's my job to keep you safe so I need to make the rule that we're not going to play Power Rangers any more. But you can still make drawings and write about them when you want."

GUIDELINE 7

Limit the use of highly structured violent toys and encourage the use of open-ended toys and play materials.

War play with highly structured and media-linked war toys generally looks quite different from war play with open-ended toys and play materials. Because highly structured or single-purpose toys are so specific in what they do (e.g., shoot darts or say mean words when a button is pushed), they define for children what they should play and how they should play (e.g., shoot, kill, and threaten). To the extent that these toys are tied to the media, they even provide scripts, defining the roles and giving children images of what they are trying to imitate. On the other hand, war toys made from open-ended materials such as clay, blocks, Legos, or a paper towel tube promote more creative play because they allow children to use them in a whole variety of ways and even to change how they're used as the play progresses.

Children often are seduced into the excitement that single-purpose combat toys appear to provide. So just "saying no" is not likely to keep these toys out of most children's lives. Few parents say they have succeeded in limiting all of the electronic and media-linked toys from their children's toy shelves, no matter how hard they try. But there is still a lot we can do.

Strategies

- *Plan toy purchases carefully and involve children in the process.* Parents can talk to other parents and relatives at gift-giving times about the kinds of toys they think would be best for their child. And when children ask for toys that are highly structured and/or violent, we need to help them gradually become more informed consumers. For instance, parents can make a list (with pictures to help with "reading") of a child's toy requests, and as a holiday approaches, they can look at the list together and discuss things like: "How would you use that toy if you had it?" "Do you think you would get bored with it once you learned what it said?" "How is it like or different from the other toys you have?" "Is there anything on the list that could help you play your favorite game in a new way?" Some guidelines to help you make good toy choices for children are provided in the chart on page 76.
- *Help children who have a lot of highly structured and electronic toys learn how to use more open-ended materials in their play.* Children who have a lot of highly structured toys can come to expect toys to tell them what to do. And then, when they are given more open-ended toys that they can control themselves and use in many ways, it can be hard for them to figure out what to do. These toys can even seem boring. Children often need help finding interesting ways to use them in their play—both at home and in group settings.

  You can introduce open-ended toys gradually to a child's single-purpose toy collection. This can help children gradually expand beyond narrowly scripted toy-controlled play. For instance, you might bring out Lego bricks to be used with "Spider-Man" action figures to build a "bed" for Spider-Man. You also may need to gradually introduce open-ended toys to children in group settings where children are used to highly structured toys.

In school settings try to keep in touch with the toys and play materials children use at home. If many are of the highly structured variety, you may find children who need help learning how to use the more open-ended kinds of toys that are found most commonly in school settings.

- *Help children move beyond the single-purpose violence often associated with war toys.* When a child uses an object such as a finger or Legos to make a weapon during war play, the initial focus for using the weapon is usually on violence and killing. For many children, this is often where the play with weapons gets stuck, and it can cause many problems with other children who get hurt or upset. It often is also the aspect of weapons play that is most disturbing to adults. By helping children get beyond this focus, the teacher can help them expand their play and avoid conflicts with other children.

For example, a child may make a Lego gun and begin shooting it at another child. The teacher can say, "Tell me how your gun works?" thereby finding out the meaning the gun has for the child. If the child were to describe the gun as one that has bullets and kills people, the teacher could say something like, "What would happen to the bad guy if your gun shot glue instead of bullets?" Or the teacher might ask, "Could this gun catch people in a different way so they would be captured, not killed?" If such questions arouse the child's interest, they could lead the child to begin to focus on ways of redesigning and/ or redefining the weapon, or they might lead the child to focus more on what will happen to the captured people (e.g., build a "prison" with blocks).

Such an intervention, when it works, achieves several things. It helps the child move beyond the notion of the single-purpose violent weapon and to expand her involvement in working with materials. It also gets her thinking about how to become involved in the issues associated with good guy/bad guy play in ways that go beyond a single focus on violence and killing.

An alternative, when this approach does not work, is to state clearly what is allowed, while giving the child an alternative way of using the toy. For instance, in the preceding situation, if the child continued to shoot bullets to kill, the teacher might say, "It is not all right to shoot at Maria when she doesn't want you to. You can shoot at the monster by the tree or you can find someone who is willing to play with you this way."

Toy Selection Guide

Try to Choose Toys That	Try to Avoid Toys That
• Can be used in a variety of ways	• Can be used only in one way
• Promote creativity and problem solving because they let children decide how they will be used	• Encourage everyone to play the same way and work on problems defined by the toy designer
• Can be enjoyed at different ages and stages	• Appeal primarily to a single age or stage
• Will continue to be fun and engaging over time	• Will sit on a shelf after the first fun 10 minutes
• Can be used with other toys to create new and more complex play opportunities	• Channel children into imitating violent scripts they see on the screen

Adapted from: *Remote Control Childhood: Combating the Hazards of Media Culture* by Diane Levin (Washington, DC: National Association for the Education of Young Children, 1998).

GUIDELINE 8

Work to counteract the highly stereotyped and limiting gender roles that characterize most war play and help children develop a broad range of roles for themselves as boys and girls.

Boys have always been more interested in this play than girls. But today, as so many of the images children see in the media and toys show extreme gender divisions—where males are strong, powerful, and love to fight, and females are weak, sexy, and need to be rescued—this difference is amplified, and we see the effects at an earlier age. Changes such as these have led Vivian Paley, an author and kindergarten teacher for many years, to say, "I am certain that superhero play begins at an earlier age than it did thirty years ago and that the boys leave the doll corner at least a year ahead of schedule."[3]

More and more, war play is an issue that separates girls from boys. In the early years, children try busily to figure out what it means to be their gender. The highly stereotyped gender divisions they see makes it very hard for children to get beyond the narrowly scripted roles they see for their gender in their play. Early segregation such as this, as well as the deep involvement of many boys in war play, can cause alienation and distrust between boys and girls and a narrowing of the range of behaviors and interests that both groups can develop. It can have potentially important effects on children's overall development as well as on their developing political attitudes.

Strategies

- *Talk with children about the gender divisions in the characters they see and bring into their play.* "Princess Leia always needs to be rescued. I wonder if there's anything else she can do to get away from the bad guys?" Or, "Does the bad guy have a family he goes home to when he's done fighting?" Or talk more directly about gender issues: "In real life, I'm glad that men don't fight like that. What do you think they could do besides fight?" It also can be helpful to use the direct experiences of children to foster reflection, evaluation, and problem solving about sex roles. This can lead to valuable discussions about segregation between the sexes in play or why boys and girls often choose to play in different areas of the room.
- *Work to expand the activities, interests, and skills of both boys and girls beyond the narrow stereotypes often modeled for them by media culture.* Try to plan activities, including play activities, that will interest both girls and boys. Help boys and girls feel comfortable trying new things.
- *Encourage interaction and friendship between girls and boys both in and out of play.* Help boys and girls join into each other's play. For instance, we saw a situation where a group of boys were building a village in outer space for the space invaders who were going around attacking earth people. The boys told a girl who asked to join in that she was not strong enough to build the village. Rather than giving a lecture on exclusion, the teacher asked the boys about their village. She saw that they were using rocks. She suggested that the girl could be the rock collector. Everyone quickly agreed, and soon several girls and then also boys were going around the playground putting rocks into a wheelbarrow. Such an approach avoided directly confronting the boys' stereotype that "girls are weaker" but at the same time gave the girls a job that was seen as using "strength."

We have heard of cases where boys who attempted to become involved in the doll corner were "shamed" out by other boys (e.g.,

"Boys don't give babies baths!"). At the same time, boys often attempt to exclude girls from their war play. An environment that implements the "Safety Rule" can help children feel safe enough to try new things.

- *Help boys get beyond the strong, powerful figures they so often imitate.* Such behaviors often can be used to mask boys' feelings of helplessness and insecurity. The boys who are most passionately involved in war play are often the ones who most need to feel powerful and who need help learning to express a range of feelings. As boys' play focuses more and more on acting out these aggressive roles to the exclusion of the dramatic play with more nurturing and feeling roles (e.g., the house corner), some boys can be cut off from a central avenue for expressing and working out feelings of vulnerability and uncertainty. We can help boys learn to express a wider range of feelings, both in their play and outside of it.

  For example, in one situation, where Seymour is about to attack Marcus for breaking his Lego gun, the adult can say, "Seymour is angry and upset because Marcus broke the gun he worked hard to build. What can we do to help Seymour feel better so he doesn't feel he needs to hit?" This response brings feelings other than power and strength into the play, gives legitimacy to them, and helps children focus on their ability to help others in nurturing ways. A similar result is accomplished if we say, "Henry is crying because you scared him when you all started running toward him growling. You were very scary monsters. Henry was trying to be a baby monster and big noises scare all kinds of babies. Who can think of a big noise that scared you when you were a baby?"

- *Provide special support to boys that do not demonstrate an interest in war play.* There will be boys who, for a variety of reasons (e.g., lack of need, exposure, and interest, or even fear of it!), will not be as caught up in war play as many of the other boys in the class. The boys who are more involved in war play can exert a great deal of both direct and indirect pressure to get these boys to join in the more aggressive war play of the group. You can build activities around the nonwar play interests that convey how important they are. For instance, if Mario is interested in doctor play because one of his parents is a doctor, setting up a hospital where the "injured" superheroes can go to be treated by Dr. Mario can help Mario become a part of the play of the boys while both maintaining his own nonwar play interest and helping the war play-focused boys to expand their play into more nurturing and diverse roles.

- *Present a variety of attractive, powerful, and humanistic role models to boys and girls so children can see alternatives to the role models that typify war play.* Providing alternative models of both males and females whom children can use in their play and discussions, such as Peter Pan and Wendy, Dorothy in *The Wizard of Oz,* Cinderella, Desmond in *Desmond and the Monsters,* and the little boy in *Abiyoyo* who helps to save the town from a terrible giant. Books like this can help both boys and girls find ways of acting powerful and strong in nonmilitaristic ways.

GUIDELINE 9

Create an ongoing dialogue between educators and parents about the children's war, weapons, and superhero play.

In any group setting with children, there will be a whole range of sentiments among teachers and parents about the issue of war play. Many parents have concerns and questions about their children's involvement in war play that generally fit into one of the two sides of the war play dilemma. They often have strong opinions also about how they would like war play to be approached with their children, both at school and at home. In addition, as teachers attempt to deal with war play more openly and actively, parents are likely to have many questions as well as potential disagreements about the teacher's approach.

Because of this, it is important that teachers and parents maintain an ongoing dialogue about war play so that both groups have the chance to explain their thoughts about the play and their rationale for the approaches they are using, and to hear the views of others. Through such discussions parents often will learn more about how to support what is happening at school and gain new insights for what to do with war play at home. They may learn effective ways to protect their children from exposure to violence and understand better why it's important to do so. Teachers also will learn a lot from dialogues with parents about children's engagement with war play, as this play can be more involved and expansive at home than at school. Listening to parents about their children's particular interests with this kind of play can give teachers new ideas about directions for the curriculum they are developing. When disagreements do arise between parents and teachers, the climate of give and take established by the dialogue will make it much more likely to come up with an approach that everyone feels they have had a part in creating.

Strategies

Create formal and informal opportunities for parents and teachers to engage in dialogue about attitudes and approaches to war play. Plan parents' nights where teachers and parents can discuss their approaches to war play and the reasons for it. Teachers can encourage parent observations in their classroom, where parents have an opportunity to see their children's war play and the teacher's role in it. Relevant articles can be made available to parents when they request additional information about war play. There are also helpful materials that can be distributed to parents like the "Questions and Answers on Dealing with War Play" in Appendix A and TRUCE Guides that are distributed by Teachers Resisting Unhealthy Children's Entertainment (see Appendix C).

Teachers and parents can discuss the particular nature of individual children's involvement in war play at parent conferences and when parents come to the class to drop off or pick up their children. Teachers can prepare classroom displays about the war play curriculum (e.g., photographs of structures made for superhero figures in the block corner). Because educational settings vary a great deal as to the amount of regular contact parents and teachers are able to have, teachers will need to develop channels of communication that are most responsive to the parents at their site.

- *Adapt what happens in the classroom, based on the information obtained from discussions with parents.* The classroom approach chosen by the teacher will be affected by the experiences the children bring to the classroom. For example, the degree to which children watch television, the degree to which commercial war toys are a part of their play at home, and the range of parent attitudes about the play will all affect the way a teacher works with individual children and the group.

- *Help parents feel supported and empowered with respect to their own roles and responsibilities in their children's war play.* Teachers can help parents feel that they have a place to come where they can discuss their feelings and concerns about war play and talk through solutions. And, as appropriate, teachers can help parents learn to facilitate their children's war play. As parents begin to discuss and become involved actively in their children's war play, they are likely to begin to feel more in control of their own feelings about this play and the influences that affect their children's lives.

- *Create an environment where parents feel comfortable talking with one another outside of school about how they deal with violent media and play.* The skills parents learn doing this also can help them talk with relatives about how to deal effectively with war play.

CONCLUSION

In this chapter we have offered a wide range of guidelines and strategies for resolving the war play dilemma in light of children's needs and current societal influences. Not all of these suggestions will work for everyone. The summary in the chart that follows can help you think about the range of possible strategies from which you can choose.

Characteristics of an Effective Approach for Resolving the War Play Dilemma

- Limits children's exposure to violent entertainment and news media as much as possible
- Ensures the safety of all the children
- Promotes the development of imaginative and creative play (rather than imitative play)
- Works to reduce dependence on highly realistic, media-linked and electronic "fighting" toys
- Encourages the use of open-ended toys and play materials
- Provides children opportunities to work out an understanding of the violence they see and hear
- Incorporates meaningful content into the play that does not depend heavily on the media
- Gives us information about children's knowledge and needs
- Counteracts the lessons they are learning about violence
- Involves children in decision making about what happens regarding war play
- Evolves as the circumstances and needs of children change
- Connects home and school

7

Resolving the War Play Dilemma: Examples of Adults and Children Working It Out Together

Reading about the issues underlying the war play dilemma, and the guidelines for how to deal with it, can make a lot of sense on paper. But transforming the ideas into action with real children is another story. Dealing with the war play dilemma is an ongoing, evolving challenge that is part of being with children today. There are no simple formulas that can be applied neatly to all situations. No two situations are ever the same. What works well in one situation may not work at all well in the next. Just when you think you understand what's going on, something may happen that throws everything into question.

So here are examples that illustrate thoughtful efforts to use the "lens" that this book provides.

MORE THAN MEETS THE EYE:
ONE FAMILY'S EFFORT TO SOLVE A WAR PLAY DILEMMA

Following is a string of e-mail correspondence Diane had with the mother of a 6-year-old son. The mother was struggling to understand and figure out how to deal with his gun play. She began this correspondence with concerns about the possible origins of the play and about the play's focus on shooting and violence. By the end, she had gained an appreciation of how her son was using the play to try to understand and deal with scary things in his world. The issues she struggles with and how she solves them illustrate graphically how many of the ideas discussed in this book really play out in practice. Diane's responses reflect her efforts to apply the principles that underlie this book to the mother's "real world."

September 18

Hi Diane

I am writing because I heard you speak at a Wheelock alumni event . . . and hope you can help me with an issue I am now having with my 6½-year-old son. Overall he's been doing well on all fronts at home and school. But one thing my husband and I have noticed lately is gun play. He never really showed an interest in it before. He watches very little TV and what he sees is carefully screened. He doesn't see the news ever, and the only thing I think he's been exposed to with guns would be the "Star Wars" movies at his grandparents' house, but that was a long, long time ago.

We've been trying to discourage the play, but he talks about it happening on the playground and with his friends. . . . I'd love to know what's "normal." Isn't he beyond the age developmentally where you'd expect to see gun play start up? I'd also like to find some suggestions for redirecting him without humiliating him with his friends or making him feel guilty if he's simply trying to "work something through."

I would really appreciate your guidance with this. Thanks.

September 20

Hello L.,

You are not alone in your concerns. Many parents voice some version of concerns similar to yours.

The fact that there is much discussion in the news right now about the United States going to war with Iraq and so many violent images around us about it makes me wonder if your son's apparent sudden interest in war play is related to the violence in the news. Kids do bring what they're hearing about in the world around them into their play. Even if he isn't hearing a lot about it at home, it may be that the children on the playground have, and he is picking it up from them. And at age 6 children do begin picking up more information from the enlarged circle of classmates first grade brings.

It's clear that you are thinking about the right basic issues regarding war play. For instance, when children engage in war play, they are often trying to work out something they heard about violence. And the more we can figure out what they're trying to work on, the more we're in a position to help. This makes your question of "why now" such an important one. It's also appropriate to question whether you should just try to squelch it because of concerns about your son's involvement with violent content. I am listing below several resources that might help you answer your questions. [See Appendix C.]

For now, my advice would be for you to try to stay connected with your son around the play and don't make him feel guilty yet! And try to figure out more about what issues/content he seems to be working on. I realize that this advice is almost always easier said than done! Good luck, and please let me know what happens.

September 21

Hi Diane

I really appreciate your getting back to me. Based on your advice I have tried to find out more about the play. I started by looking more closely at what's happening with my son and his friends' play.

We live in a neighborhood with three other 6- to 7-year-old boys. They all play together regularly. I've become fascinated by what the other parents do about gun play. They represent all possible approaches to dealing with it!

One mom who just recently moved here teaches "safety" stuff to her son by being up front and blatantly honest. She talks about real guns and how they hurt people, and abductions and how to protect yourself from kidnappers. She tells him it's not okay to even pretend to hurt anyone. Her son seems a bit desensitized, but scared (he has separation anxiety and has trouble trying new things).

Another mom has tons of toy guns and even has bb guns for her boys. Her son. . . . has been seen hiding in the bushes aiming a toy gun at one of the other boys, with whom he'd had a fight.

The third mom was surprised when I said there'd been gun play, saying her son "never does that." Yet her 10-year-old daughter heard her and said, "Mom, they do it all the time!"

Poor kids. I know they're all just struggling to figure the world out, and they're probably hopelessly confused by the variety of messages they get from home.

I agree with trying to avoid having my son feel guilt and shame about his play. I remember your telling a story when I heard you speak, about your own struggle to allow your son to live in a world of peers yet guide him in his behavior and choices. It involved going to a movie that most of his friends had seen. I appreciated hearing that even an expert struggles with these issues, and also that there often isn't one simple, right answer.

Again, thank you for your help. I will write more as the situation develops.

October 4

Dear L.,

Your description of the approaches of the other mothers in your neighborhood graphically captures the range of approaches parents use to deal with war play today. It also captures so well the complexities of what happens when the children from all the different approaches come together!! Please keep writing to me.

October 8

Hi Diane,

Thanks so much. It's helpful to be reassured that parents universally struggle over the kinds of issues we're dealing with.

Happily, things have calmed down a lot since I last wrote and I think I know why: *My husband and I have changed our approach.* Now, instead of looking the other way or saying, "No guns," we ask our son about *why* he's shooting and using guns—for instance, "What do you need that gun for? What's the problem?" This has led to a lot more discussion and exploration of the theme.

My son actually went into detail about "bad guys" and how "it could happen anytime, Mom!" Puzzled, I asked what he meant and he explained that "they" [the bad guys] could come into our house at any time and take our stuff or hurt us [apparently real fears at present]. In his fantasies he had worked out how "they" might get into the house—through his second floor window—without figuring out that they'd need a ladder!

Something is clearly going on. He probably is hearing more fearful info given his recent foray into the real world via first grade and widespread presence of war and terrorism stories in the news. But I had this "aha" experience when I suddenly connected with a big item in the news this summer—children being kidnapped, especially the child in California who was taken from her bedroom! There has also been talk around here this past summer about a couple of abduction attempts which I know the kids are talking about. His descriptions and his play seemed connected to the news.

It really helped to look at his war play as being connected to this fear. We have tried to reassure him that he is safe. We told him that our two dogs would protect him at all costs so he didn't have to worry that "they" would get in. Still he held on to his fear.

Then, we found something that really did work. I have a friend who lived in Japan and she brought me back a pair of gargoyles that the Japanese put on either side of their door to protect homes. I figured I'd try bringing them out and share the folklore with my son. We agreed to put them on the floor outside his and his sister's bedroom doors. The very next morning my son entered our room and said with a big smile, "It worked!" and he's slept well every night since then. And at the moment the gun play seems to be less intense. He seems more interested in other favorite play themes and leisure activities.

This has been a very helpful journey. Now I realize he'll be facing bad stuff all his life, and it'll be an ongoing struggle to help him and his sister make sense of their lives. But now I'm feeling a bit more confident about helping them. Thanks again.

October 9

Hello L.,

Thank you for sharing your amazing account of what has happened with A's gun play! It's so important that you succeeded in figuring out what was underlying the play as well as a way to help him feel safe that worked for him. And what a unique and creative solution! It's one that connected to the concrete way he thinks about the world, not to adult logic. I worry that many children have such fears and never get a chance to get the help they need dealing with them.

Please keep in touch with any additional developments with your son.

This mother's breakthrough realization that her son's unexpected interest in gun play probably was connected in some way to several abductions of children that recently had figured prominently in the news, led her to find a new way of thinking about and dealing with her son and his gun play.

It's often hard to figure out how to talk to children about war play in a way that opens up the conversation rather than sounding judgmental or preachy. It is also hard to raise some of the important issues about guns and violence that you'd like to discuss. To assist you in having such conversations with children that are well-matched to their level of understanding, Nancy wrote the following letter, which is used by the organization of teachers called TRUCE. It can be read to children as a way to help them start thinking about the issues.

Dear Children,

Some kids really love toy guns and toys with weapons on them. They have fun pretending to fight with them. A lot of teachers worry about weapon toys. They think that if kids play with these toys and pretend to fight and kill, it will teach kids that it's okay to hurt people and that fighting and hurting is fun. Kids often say, "We're only pretending. We're just 'playing.'"

Some teachers say kids in their classes pretend to be characters on TV. Kids act out kicking and fighting. Then kids often really do hurt each other. It gets scary. It isn't pretend, teachers say. Many teachers are worried. They are angry that TV shows and ads make violent toys look cool so kids want to buy them. They think companies shouldn't use TV programs to sell violent toys to kids.

- What do you think about what the teachers say?
- What do you think teachers, parents, and children should do about fighting toys?
- What can grown-ups do to help children be safe and learn not to fight?
- What ideas do you have about how children can play without fighting toys?

From Many Teachers All Over the Country[1]

USING A CLASS MEETING TO TAME THE POWER RANGERS: WORKING WITH CHILDREN TO SOLVE THE WAR PLAY DILEMMA

In the following scenario, a teacher shows us how a whole group of children can be involved in working out a solution to an ongoing problem with war play that has a lot of the children upset. It illustrates the process we can use to create a safe and caring environment for children where they can work together to solve problems that are important to them. It also shows how we can help children become more reflective about their war play as well as take more responsibility for their actions. Furthermore, the very approach models for children a way of being together and working out problems that does not involve violence. This is exactly what we need to teach in order to counteract the lessons the violence in their war play can teach. The situation is as follows:

> Several kindergarten children are playing outside in a large appliance carton covered in aluminum foil. Suddenly, three boys race over and begin to karate chop and kick the box. Just as a teacher comes over to deal with the resulting commotion, a child in the box reaches a fist out and hits an "attacker," who bursts into tears crying, "But, I'm a Power Ranger!"

This isn't the first time this teacher has dealt with a crisis created by the presence of Power Rangers in the classroom. After dealing with the immediate problem, she decides it's time to bring the issue to a class meeting so all the children can work on a solution together. In the following class discussion we have inserted comments that highlight key elements of the conversation related to resolving the war play dilemma.

Teacher: I've noticed a problem and I need your help figuring out how to solve it. You know how a lot of children have been playing Power Rangers outside lately? [Several children nod agreement.] Well, when you play Power Rangers it doesn't feel safe. It ends up with someone getting upset, or hurt. . . even, crying. Often it's not even someone who was playing. What ideas do you have about it?

Jenna: I hate them. I never play.

What's happening?

- The teacher *states the problem* by referring to the children's recent direct experience.
- To help them connect cause and effect, she explains in concrete ways how children are affected by the play.
- She acknowledges there is more than one side to the problem.
- She focuses on keeping the children *safe* rather than casting blame.
- After she explains the problem, she brings children into the discussion where they voice their opinions about the problem.

Teacher: Yes, you really don't like to play Power Rangers and I've seen you get unhappy when children playing them go near you. Who has ideas about what happens when children who are playing go near those who aren't playing?

- She acknowledges Jenna's comment, and then tries to get the children to elaborate on their understanding of the problem.

Camilla: A fight.
Jenna: I always go to a teacher.
Raymond: I hit them if they bother me. That stops 'em!

- Young children often focus on the *concrete* actions and salient aspects of experiences.

Teacher: Fighting, running to a teacher, and hitting are usually things to do when you don't feel safe. What do the Power Rangers do that doesn't feel safe?

- Without making a value judgment, she shows the causal connections between feelings and actions.
- She keeps relating children's comments to a basic goal for the classroom—for everyone to feel safe.

Raymond: They messed up the spaceship today.
Lai Ling: They're too mean.
Teacher: Can you tell us more about how they are mean?

- She tries to get Lai Ling to focus on the concrete aspects of Power Rangers' behavior and how their actions affect others.

Lai Ling: They yell in your face, and they kick and punch. I hate them!
Teacher: So you *really* don't like their noise and their kicking.

- She highlights for everyone what about the Power Rangers' behavior creates the problem.

Karlos: But that's what Power Rangers do. They NEEEED to fight.
Teacher: So it sounds like there is a problem. The children playing Power Rangers like to play fight, but other children don't like it when the Power Rangers come near them.

- Without expressing a value judgment, she shows how this is a shared problem with two sides. This can help the children get beyond their egocentric viewpoint.

Teacher: It's hard to feel safe when all that fighting and noise is near you and you're trying to do something else. We need to find something to do about the Power Rangers so everyone feels safe. Does anyone have any ideas about how we could do that?

- She again relates the problem to the need for everyone's safety and shows exactly what makes the children not feel safe.
- Once the problem is clarified, she quickly moves things on to working on *possible solutions.* She reminds the children that feeling safe is the most important requirement of any solution.

Sammy: Play somewhere else.
Teacher: You mean Power Rangers play away from other children?
        [Sammy nods.]
Riannan: Use your words.
Teacher: So what are some of the words you could use?

- Serving as a translator, she focuses on *how each solution might work* in action.

Mark: Say, "Go away."
Gilda: Say, "Don't hit" or "Be quiet."
Henry: Say, "No play fighting at school"—like we did at my day care.
Karlos: Oh, brother. [There are a few other groans.]
Teacher: Karlos, it sounds like you don't like that idea. Tell us more.

- By picking up on his groan, the teacher shows differing viewpoints will be respected. This promotes a sense of independence and trust.

Karlos: They need to fight. That's what they do.

- Karlos is comfortable saying what he thinks, rather than what he thinks the teacher wants to hear.

Teacher: I wonder if there are other things they could do besides fight?

- She wants to help the children expand their repertoire of ideas about what the Power Rangers can do beyond the narrow focus on violence.

Hung Mo: They go to high school.

Jenna: They eat in a big room.
Darcy: Hey. The Power Rangers could eat at our restaurant! [Currently in the dramatic play area.]

- This is the kind of unpredictable breakthrough that can come from a group problem-solving session. It creates a solution that expands Power Ranger play beyond just fighting.

Teacher: You've really worked hard on this problem and come up with a lot of good ideas. Let's try some of them tomorrow to see how they work. Power Rangers, what if we choose a special place where you can play outside away from the others? Do you think you could try that? [Several nod.] And children in the restaurant, do you think you can make a meal for the Power Rangers? They must get really hungry. [More nods.]

- The teacher sees fidgeting so she tries to bring closure by choosing two of the solutions that she thinks *everyone can agree* to and will *promote safety.*
- As she shows how the two solutions take into account both sides of the problem, she makes sure all the children agree to her proposal.
- She also helps them see what they need to do to begin *translating both solutions into practice.*

Hung Mo: But it better be something we like to eat!

- He shows he has already begun to think about concrete ways he can put the solution into practice.

Teacher: [Nods and smiles.] You've been sitting for a long time. Let's try these two new ideas. I like that the Power Rangers will have something to do besides fighting. We'll talk about how things go at our end-of-day meeting tomorrow.

- Here the teacher does bring in a personal opinion about fighting.
- She ends when she is sure the children have a definite plan they all agreed to try in order to solve their problem.
- She also helps the children think ahead and know that they will have a chance to *evaluate their solutions* after they have tried them out.

And if the Problem Continues

What if the children try out their solutions and the problems with the Power Ranger play continue? This might be a time for the teacher to implement *Option 5—"Limit the War Play but Provide Alternative Ways to Work on the Issues.* She could do this by holding another meeting and telling the children that she feels she has to ban the Power Ranger play because they haven't been able to find a way to "have the play *and* keep everyone safe." She then can have a give-and-take conversation about other things the children who like the Power Rangers can do outside of their play—like draw pictures or have special meeting times when they can talk about them. She also might ask for ideas about what could help the children who like to play Power Rangers remember not to engage in that play. This could start a whole new line of discussion about other interesting things to do or interesting themes to play.

This teacher's approach to problem solving can be used to work out all sorts of war play-related problems with children—at school and at home. For instance, beyond using it as a way to create "rules" for the play that promote safety and learning, it can also help you work out what toys to buy and which television programs to watch and how many. The following chart summarizes the five key components involved in having such a discussion with children.

Five-Part, Problem-Solving Process for Working with Children

- *Talk about the problem* (what happened) in terms the children can understand.
- *Come up with possible solutions* and talk about how each one might work or not work in practice.
- *Choose a solution* that everyone involved can agree to try because in takes into account their ideas, issues, and concerns.
- *Try out the solution and see how it works* by directly experiencing the consequences.
- *Evaluate how the solution worked* and decide whether and how to change it to make it work better.

CONCLUSION

Can We Resolve the War Play Dilemma? Creating a Better World for Children and Their Play

Children have engaged in war and weapons play for generations. It is a form of play that can help them work on issues that are basic to their development and to the ideas they build about their world. Society, by the images and models it provides, influences what children will use in their war play and the lessons they will learn. Therefore, any consideration of war play today cannot occur without considering the widespread violence that permeates society, especially the violence that is marketed to children by the entertainment industry. We have tried to show throughout this book how serious a problem the marketing of violence to children has become. It is harming what, when, and how children play and what they learn from their play.

The violent images that surround today's children penetrate classrooms and homes, often against the wishes of adults. Parents' and teachers' attempts to limit war play often meet with difficulty. Teachers who ban the play talk about an underworld that develops as children try to continue their war play outside of adults' view—in whispers in the reading loft, or with action figures pulled out of pockets under the platform on the playground. Parents who try to curb their children's war play say they have difficulty maintaining this position as their children are exposed to violent television programs and war toys from many different directions. They say it is impossible to avoid the inundation of violent images—on pajamas or lunchboxes, in toy advertisements enclosed in the Sunday paper, on television screens, and at airports and shopping malls.

Along with voicing their own frustration and lack of control, teachers and parents often look to one another to do something to improve the situation. Often, early childhood professionals criticize parents for allowing their children to watch violent programs on television and buy toys and products associated with these shows, play video games, and see films rated for older children. They call on parents to "just turn the television off and draw the line"; to "just say 'no'" to their children.

And in return, parents often point the finger at schools and group settings as the source of their children's first interest in violent play. They make such comments as, "My son never heard of Power Rangers or wanted a toy gun until he went to school." But, increasingly in recent years, both parents and early childhood educators have been placing more and more of the blame on toy manufacturers and the entertainment industry as a major contributor to children's current preoccupation with violence and war play.

In response to parents' and early childhood professionals' charges, representatives of the toy industry frequently assert that the marketplace governs toy-manufacturing patterns. They say that parents know what is best for their children and that they would not make the toys "if parents didn't buy them." They do not discuss the millions of dollars they spend marketing their products to children in increasingly sophisticated ways, or the strategies they use to create an environment that undermines parents' authority and control over what gets into their children's lives.

When it comes to making marketing decisions, the industry too often seems to use the criterion of whether a product is "in demand" and will sell, and not what is in the best interests of children, families, schools, or society. Any negative effects are not reflected in the industries' profit-and-loss calculations and thus do not guide their decisions. But ideally, we would live in a society that supports parents' attempts to raise healthy, productive, socially responsible children. Instead, the entertainment and toy industries actually undermine parents' efforts at every turn. Their immense power (and profit) often is gained at the expense of those who most care about children's well-being.

We have shown in Part III of this book that there is a great deal that parents and early childhood educators can do to counteract the harm caused by all of the violence in children's lives that so often shapes their play; and, there is much they can do to encourage children's healthy development and play. However, until we change the environment that allows "for fun" violence to be marketed so freely to children and that so permeates and influences their war play, the war play dilemma will not be fully resolved.

We believe, therefore, that there are compelling grounds for public-sector policies that will help regain some degree of balance of power between children's and corporate interests. Many other countries have already struck a better balance. Sweden and Norway have successful voluntary restrictions on the sale of war toys; Malta prohibits their import; Greece bans television advertising directed to children; Australia places some restrictions on imports of war toys. The European Parliament recommended that its member states ban advertising of war toys and reduce their sale. But in the United States, government has yet to live up to its responsibility to care for and protect the nation's children from the ever-increasing market forces that push violence. The price children will pay for society's failure to meet their needs will be paid ultimately by everyone.

In the years that we have been studying the war play dilemma, we have collected countless examples of creative steps, large and small, taken by people at every level of society to improve the current situation for children. These stories have convinced us that there is much we can do, must do, to work to create a society that better supports our efforts to promote children's positive social and political development than is currently the case. And we would like to end this book by urging every one of you not only to work with children to deal with the war play dilemma, but also to work to change the conditions in society that make war play such a dilemma for us all, especially for children.

Appendix A

Questions and Answers on Dealing with War Play

The questions and answers that follow were created as a concise handout on war play to be used at workshops sponsored by the *ACT Training Program,* a joint project of the American Psychological Association (APA) and the National Association for the Education of Young Children. Diane Levin with Julia Silva, Director of the ACT Program at the APA, prepared the text. Schools, child care centers, PTAs, and other organizations working with young children and their parents have found it helpful to distribute.

1. Is it harmful for children to play with toys that are associated with aggression like toy knives, swords, or guns? Many parents and teachers worry when children bring toy guns or other toy weapons into their play. There is no simple answer. Children use their play to work out, express, and master their experiences—in the family, school, and neighborhood, and with the media—and if they see real or pretend violence and weapons, they may bring that to their play. Weapons play is also one way children try to meet their need to feel strong and powerful. But not all weapons play is the same, and it is important to look at the nature of the play to figure out whether it is harmful to children. For play to have a positive effect, it needs to be controlled by the child, show creativity and imagination, and change over time. That is what happened in much of the weapons play and other play in the past, when children played cops and robbers. But it has changed dramatically in recent years with children increasingly exposed to guns and fighting in the news, TV programs, films, and video and computer games, and to "toys of violence" marketed through TV programs and films. Play has become mostly imitative—the play with violence often imitates TV scripts. Children often have little opportunity to use creativity and imagination to work out their own ideas about situations, which is necessary for them to do in order to meet their developmental needs. This kind of weapons play can be harmful to children and may contribute to the development of aggressive behaviors.

2. What should adults do if children spontaneously use their fingers or an object to represent a weapon? Don't panic! Make sure everyone is safe. Then, watch the weapons play to learn more about what the children are struggling to understand and what may be worrying them. Look at how creative and imaginative or imitative and repetitive the play seems to be, whether it changes over time, and whether it stays focused primarily on violence. Try to keep channels of communication open with children both during and after the play. Help them come up with ways to extend the play, for instance, with more open-ended toys and props such as rescue vehicles and medical equipment or simple discussions about what could happen next. Ask questions about the play without making children feel guilty. Try to follow the children's lead in the roles that you take rather than taking over the play. If the play gets scary or dangerous, gently intervene and redirect it. For example, ask children, "How could people help one another?" Or provide alternative toys. Stop the play if your efforts are failing to keep them safe. Once the play is over, talk to the children about it. Reassure them about their safety. Answer questions simply. Clear up confusions. Talk about alternatives to the harmful lessons children may be learning about violence, for instance, by asking if there is another way the characters could have solved their problem besides fighting or what would they do in "real life" if they had such a problem.

APPENDIX B

Two Sample Curriculum Webs

In this appendix we present two sample curriculum webs, one using *The Wizard of Oz* and the other developing themes around children's play focused on creatures from outer space. Such curriculum webs can be useful to teachers in a number of ways. They can assist in keeping track of activities that occur as well as in planning what might happen next. They provide a technique for quickly recording and organizing a great deal of information about a curriculum or play theme in a visually clear and easy-to-read fashion. No two webs will ever look the same; the information in the web will depend on the particular setting, and the categories used and connections made among categories will depend on the reason and functions of the web.

For example, a web may be used to record information about what has occurred around a theme, around subject areas, or around teacher interventions; to plan for a new theme; to further activities that have already occurred; or to plan for one child, based on what she or he has already done. Weaving webs on a regular basis (e.g., weekly, or at the beginning, middle, and end of a particular theme) can provide systematic documentation of the curriculum as well as a regular procedure for curriculum development. Teachers might work together in making webs; in that case, the web making provides a way to share information quickly that each teacher obtained and to plan for shared objectives and responses. Teachers might share their webs with parents, to give an overview of what has been occurring in the classroom related to war play, as well as the range of activities, learning, and issues that might have been involved.

The process of making a curriculum web is usually as important as the product obtained, because of the organizing of information that occurs as it is made. The first few attempts are often the most challenging because it can be difficult at first to brainstorm in a free and nonlinear manner, breaking away from the more familiar approach of organizing information in a linear and logical fashion (e.g., a series of lessons).

The following two curriculum webs illustrate these points.

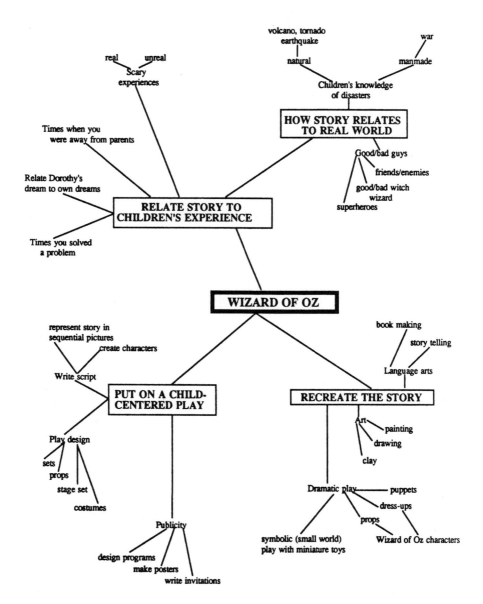

volcano, tornado
earthquake

war

natural

manmade

real   unreal
Scary
experiences

Children's knowledge
of disasters

**HOW STORY RELATES
TO REAL WORLD**

Times when you
were away from parents

Good/bad guys

friends/enemies

good/bad witch
wizard

superheroes

Relate Dorothy's
dream to own dreams

**RELATE STORY TO
CHILDREN'S EXPERIENCE**

Times you solved
a problem

WIZARD OF OZ

represent story in
sequential pictures

book making

create characters

story telling

Write script

Language arts

**PUT ON A CHILD-
CENTERED PLAY**

RECREATE THE STORY

Art

painting

Play design

drawing

sets

clay

props

stage set

Dramatic play

puppets

costumes

dress-ups

props

Publicity

symbolic (small world)
play with miniature toys

Wizard of Oz characters

design programs
make posters

write invitations

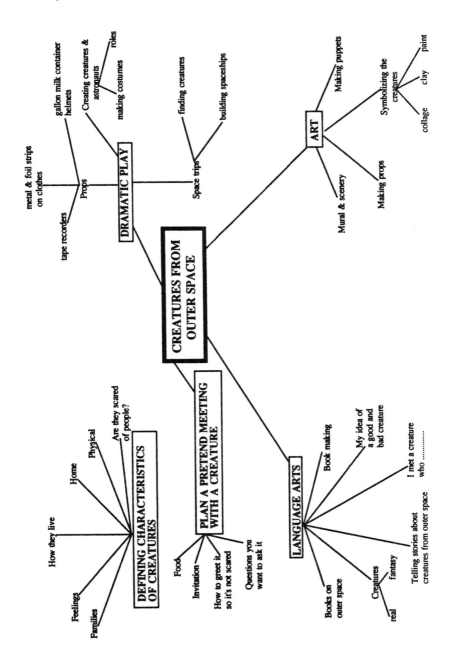

APPENDIX C

Resources for Working on the War Play Dilemma

FURTHER READING FOR ADULTS

American Medical Association. (1996). *Physician guide to media violence.* Chicago: Author.
Reader-friendly summary of research on the impact of media violence on children and what can be done about it.

Bay, W. (2003). *Talking to your kids in tough times: How to answer your child's questions about the world we live in.* New York: Warner.
Helps adults talk with children about a wide range of disturbing issues (including violence) that children often bring into their play.

Berk, L. (1994, November). Vygotsky's theory: The importance of make-believe play. *Young Children, 50*(1), 30–39.
Readable article showing key aspects of Lev Vygotsky's theory about children's play and its value to healthy development.

Bronson, M. (1995). *The right stuff for children birth to 8: Selecting play materials to support development.* Washington, DC: National Association for the Education of Young Children.
Overview of traditional play materials and the positive role they can serve in play and development.

Cantor, J. (1998). *"Mommy, I'm scared!" How TV and movies frighten children and what we can do to protect them.* New York: Harcourt Brace.
Reader-friendly discussion of the harm caused to children by media violence and how we can make it better.

Carlsson-Paige, N., & Levin, D. E. (1990). *Who's calling the shots? How to respond effectively to children's fascination with war play and war toys.* Gabriola Island, BC: New Society Publishers.

Practical parenting book on why and how war play has changed, how the changes are harming children, and how to work with children to counteract the harm.

Carlsson-Paige, N., & Levin, D. E. (1992, Winter). The subversion of healthy development and play: Teachers' reactions to the Teenage Mutant Ninja Turtles. *Day Care & Early Education, 19*(2), 14–20.
One of the few studies of how violent media linked to violent toys is affecting children's behavior and play in school.

Carlsson-Paige, N., & Levin, D. (1998). *Before push comes to shove: Building conflict resolution skills with children.* St. Paul, MN: Redleaf Press. [Also see accompanying children's book, *Best Day of the Week* by N. Carlsson-Paige.]
A practical guide (to be used with or without the children's book) on how ideas about conflict resolution develop and what we can do to nurture them.

Carlsson, U., & von Feilitzen, C. (Eds.). (1998). *Children and media violence: Yearbook for the UNESCO International Clearinghouse on Children & Violence on the Screen.* Goteborg, Sweden: UNESCO International Clearinghouse on Children & Violence on the Screen.
A comprehensive look at media violence and its impact on children at a global level from a United Nations-linked organization that serves as a clearinghouse on media issues.

Child Magazine. (2003). *Feeling safe: Talking to children about war and terrorism.* New York: Barnes & Noble.
Written to help adults talk with their children about the issues that come up in this post-September 11th world.

Cross, G. (1997). *Toys and the changing world of American childhood.* Cambridge, MA: Harvard University Press.
Examines the history and role of toys, and how both are changing today.

DeGaetano, G. (2004). *Parenting well in a media age: Keeping our kids human.* Fawnskin, CA: Personhood Press.
Helps parents raise healthy children in the midst of the commercial, media-driven culture that surrounds them.

Developmental Studies Center. (1996). *Ways we want our class to be.* Oakland, CA: Author.
Shows how to create classrooms that empower children to be responsible and caring participants in learning. [Also see accompanying film by the same name.]

Dyson, A. (1997). *Writing superheroes: Contemporary childhood, popular culture, and classroom literacy.* New York: Teachers College Press.
Explores how children use their writing to work on some of the same kind of content as in war play—and work on literacy learning at the same time.

Egenfeldt-Nielsen, S., & Smith, J. H. (2004). *Playing with fire: How do computer games influence the player?* Goteborg, Sweden: Nordicom.
Succinct summary of what is known about the nature and impact of computer games on children and youth around the world.

Feinburg, S. G. (1973). *Combat in child art.* New York: Norton.
Case study analysis of the role of combat art in helping children work on similar issues as in war play.

Freud, A., & Burlingham, D. T. (1943). *War and children.* New York: Ernst Willard.
Classic book about the psychological impact of World War II on children in England, including an analysis of war play.

Fromberg, D., & Bergen, D. (Eds.). (in press). *Play from birth to twelve: Contexts, perspectives, and meanings* (2nd ed.). New York: Garland Press.
A comprehensive anthology of essays by experts in the play field on the far-reaching importance of play and contemporary issues affecting it.

Garbarino, J. (1995). *Raising children in a socially toxic environment.* San Francisco: Jossey-Bass.
Critique of the factors in society that are contributing to the stresses of parenting today.

Grossman, D., & DeGaetano, G. (1999). *Stop teaching our kids to kill: A call to action against TV, movie and video game violence.* New York: Crown.
Critique of violent video games and how they desensitize children to violence.

Groves, B. (2002). *Children who see too much: Lessons from the Child Witness to Violence Project.* Boston: Beacon Press.
Valuable book about the ways in which witnessing violence can affect children and how adults can help them.

Hoffman, D. (2004). *Magic capes, amazing powers: Transforming superhero play in the classroom.* St. Paul, MN: Redleaf Press.
In-depth look at superhero play in the classroom, the passion behind it, and how teachers can harness it.

Jones, J. (2002). *Killing monsters: Why children need fantasy, super heroes, and make-believe violence.* New York: Basic Books.
Misuses the developmental side of the war play debate to argue that today's media provide children with the content they need to work out power, fear, and safety issues.

Katch, J. (2001). *Under deadman's skin: Discovering the meaning of children's violent play.* Boston: Beacon Press.
In the style of Vivian Paley, a revealing account of how 5- and 6-year-old children act out violence, with suggestions for how to reduce violent influences on them.

Katch, J. (2003). They don't like me: Lessons on bullying and teasing from a preschool classroom. Boston: Beacon Press.
A gripping account of one teacher's efforts to understand and work with the bullying behavior in her classroom.

Koplow, L. (Ed.). (1996). *Unsmiling faces: How preschools can heal.* New York: Teachers College Press.
Valuable book for understanding the emotional lives of young children; offers a framework for including and healing emotions and trauma in the classroom.

Kreidler, W., & Whitall, S. (1999). *Adventures in peacemaking: A conflict resolution guide for early childhood educators* (2nd ed.). Cambridge, MA: Educators for Social Responsibility.
Activity guide to help early childhood caregivers teach young children nonviolent ways to resolve conflicts.

Levin, D. E. (1996). Endangered play, endangered development: A constructivist view of the role of play in development and learning. In A. Phillips (Ed.), *Playing for keeps* (pp. 73–88). St. Paul, MN: Redleaf Press.
A critique of the importance of play, how society is currently undermining its development, and the harm this is causing children's development, learning, and behavior.

Levin, D. E. (1998). *Remote control childhood? Combating the hazards of media culture.* Washington, DC: National Association for the Education of Young Children.
A comprehensive media literacy guide about what we can do to promote positive development and learning in today's media culture.

Levin, D. E. (2003). *Teaching young children in violent times: Building a peaceable classroom* (2nd ed.). Cambridge, MA: Educators for Social Responsibility and Washington, DC: National Association for the Education of Young Children.
Provides developmentally based, practical strategies for counteracting the harmful lessons our violent society is teaching children and sample conversations on talking with kids about conflict and violence issues.

Levin, D. E. (2003). When the world is a dangerous place. *Educational Leadership, 60*(7), 72–75.
Provides the information that educators need to play an active role in helping children process violence in the news.

Levin, D. E. (2005). "So sexy, so soon: The sexualization of childhood." In S. Olfman (Ed.), *Childhood lost: How American culture is failing our kids* (pp. 137–153). Westport, CT: Praeger Press.
Critical look at how sex, like violence, is used as a marketing tool with children and the problems this creates for children's gender development, images of themselves, and relationships with others.

Levin, D. E., & Carlsson-Paige, N. (1995, September). The "Mighty Morphin Power Rangers": Teachers voice concern. *Young Children, 50*(6), 67–72.

Documents and discusses teachers' concerns about the impact of children's programs like the Power Rangers on their children and classrooms.

Levin, D. E., & Carlsson-Paige, N. (2004, February). Marketing violence: The special toll on young children of color. *Journal of Negro Education* [Theme issue on commercialism and children of color], *62*(4), 427–437.
Discusses the special hazards that marketing of violence for children of color.

Levine, M. L. (1998). See no evil: A guide to protecting our children from media violence. San Francisco: Jossey-Bass.
Helpful guide showing how media violence affects each stage of a child's development and aiding parents in their search for healthy and age-appropriate television programs and films.

Linn, S. (2004). *Consuming kids: The hostile takeover of childhood.* New York: New Press.
Issues a wake-up call for parents about marketing to children in our consumer culture and how it is shaping children's lives.

Olfman, S. (Ed.). (2003). *All work and no play . . . how educational reforms are harming our preschoolers.* Westport, CT: Greenwood/Praeger.
Valuable collection of essays on the importance of play and how play is endangered because of academic pressures on young children.

Olfman, S. (Ed.). (2005). *Childhood lost: How American culture is failing our kids.* Westport, CT: Greenwood/Praeger.
Collection of essays on the range of ways contemporary society is undermining children's health, development, and behavior.

Paley, V. G. (1984). *Bad guys don't have birthdays: Fantasy play at four.* Chicago: University of Chicago Press.
Charming book that shows the fantasy life of kindergarten children and the vital role of fantasy play in their healthy development.

Paley, V. G. (1984). *Boys and girls: Superheroes in the doll corner.* Chicago: University of Chicago Press.
Delightful book about the superhero play of boys and the domestic play of girls, its meaning for children, and implications for the adults who work with them.

Piaget, J. (1951). *Play, dreams, and imitation in childhood.* New York: Norton. (Original French edition published 1945)
Theoretical study of the evolution of imitation and play in childhood and how these develop and change in the early years.

Piaget, J. (1965). *The moral judgement of the child.* New York: Free Press. (Original French edition published 1932)
Classic study of child morality, including children's ideas about rules, lying,

cheating, adult authority, punishment, and responsibility, and how their attitudes toward these change throughout the early years.

Pollack, W. (1998). *Real boys: Rescuing our sons from the myths of boyhood.* New York: Random House.
Illuminating book that helps parents and other adults hear and respond to the needs of growing boys.

Ravitch, D., & Viteritti, J. (2003). *Kids stuff: Marketing sex and violence to America's children.* Baltimore, MD: Johns Hopkins University Press.
A collection of essays about the toxic nature of today's media, with suggestions for solutions that can provide the guidance children need.

Ready by 5. (1995). *Moving young children's play away from TV violence.* Baltimore, MD: Author.

Ready by 5. (1998). *Bring parents into the picture.* Baltimore, MD: Author. [Companion to above].
These two books provide information and strategies for dealing with war play in group settings and homes.

Rideout, V., Vandewater, E., & Wartella, E. (Fall, 2003). *Zero to six: Electronic media in the lives of infants, toddlers and preschoolers.* Menlo Park, CA: Kaiser Family Foundation Report.
The first publicly released national study of media use among very young children (from 6 months to 6 years old).

Schor, J. (2005). *Born to buy: The commercialized child and the new consumer culture.* New York: Scribner.
An eye-opening book that reveals how marketers exploit children and youth for profit and the devastating effects this has on young people.

Steyer, J. (2002). *The other parent.* New York: Atria Books.
Readable book about how media are bombarding children today and how parents can counter these images and influences.

Terr, L. C. (1990). *Too scared to cry: Psychic trauma in childhood.* New York: Harper & Row.
Breakthrough book that identified the special impact traumatic experiences can have on children's play.

Vance, E., & Weaver, P. J. (2002). *Class meetings: Young children solving problems together.* Washington, DC: National Association for the Education of Young Children.
Provides useful information and examples of how to talk with groups of children about issues of shared concern.

Wheeler, E. (2004). *Conflict resolution in early childhood: Helping children understand and resolve conflicts.* Englewood Cliffs, NJ: Prentice-Hall.
A comprehensive examination of what we know about how children learn conflict resolution and what we can do to help them.

ORGANIZATIONS DEALING WITH WAR PLAY
AND RELATED ISSUES

Alliance for Childhood

P.O. Box 444, College Park, MD 20741
(301) 779–1033; www.allianceforchildhood.net
Promotes policies and practices that support children's healthy
development and play.

American Academy of Pediatrics

141 Northwest Point Boulevard, Elk Grove Village, IL 60007
(847) 434–4000; www.aap.org
Prepares position statements and informational pamphlets for
pediatricians and the public on media violence and popular culture
issues.

American Psychological Association

750 First Street, NE, Washington, DC 20002–4242
(800) 374–2721; www.apa.org
Sponsors Adults and Children Together Against Violence (ACT), a
community-based early childhood violence prevention program,
which distributes the "Questions and Answers on Dealing with
War Play" brochure for parents and early childhood educators in
Appendix A. www.actagainstviolence.org

Campaign for a Commercial-Free Childhood

Judge Baker Children's Center, Harvard Medical School,
53 Parker Hill Avenue, Boston, MA
(617) 278–4105; www.commercialfreechildhood.org
Coalition working to stop marketing practices that harm children.

Center for Media Literacy

3101 Ocean Park Boulevard, Suite 200, Santa Monica, CA 90495
(800) 228–4630; www.medialit.org
Best catalog of media literacy materials, including media literacy
curriculum, *Beyond Blame*.

Coalition for Quality Children's Video and Kids First

112 W. San Francisco Street, Suite 305A, Santa Fe, NM 87501
(505) 989–8076; www.cqcm.org/kidsfirst
Promotes and rates children's videos.

Commercial Alert

3719 SE Hawthorne Boulevard, #281, Portland, OR 97214
(501) 235–8012; www.commercialalert.org
Advocates for policies to limit harmful marketing and
commercialism directed at children.

Common Sense Media

500 Treat Avenue, Suite 100, San Francisco, CA 94110
(415) 643–6300; www.commonsensemedia.org
Provides resources for wise media use with children, including up-
to-date reviews and ratings based on developmental criteria and
materials for parent workshops.

Concerned Educators Allied for a Safe Environment (CEASE)

52 Frost Street, Cambridge, MA 02140
www.peaceeducators.org
National network of parents and educators working to educate
the public about global issues that harm children, including war
play.

Educators for Social Responsibility

23 Garden Street, Cambridge, MA 02138
(617) 492–1764; www.esrnational.org
Promotes peace curriculum in school systems. Produces and
distributes curriculum material on peace education issues (preschool
through high school).

National Association for the Education of Young Children

1509 16th Street, NW, Washington, DC 20036
(202) 232–8777; (800) 424–2460; www.naeyc.org
Provides many resources for professionals and parents, including
books, pamphlets, posters, and a journal (*Young Children*).

National Institute on Media & the Family

2450 Riverside Avenue, Minneapolis, MN 55454
(888) 672-KIDS; www.mediaandthefamily.org
Newsletter rating media products' impact on children; produces
media literacy materials.

Playing for Keeps

116 West Illinois, Suite 5E, Chicago, IL 60610
(877) 755–5347; www.playingforkeeps.org
Dedicated to improving quality of life and learning for children by
promoting healthy and constructive play.

Teachers Resisting Unhealthy Children's Entertainment (TRUCE)

P.O. Box 441261, W. Somerville, MA 02144
www.truceteachers.org; e-mail: truceteachers@aol.com
Educators who prepare "Toy Action Guide," "Media Violence Action
Guide" and other free guides for parents.

TV-Turnoff Network

1200 29th Street, NW, Washington, DC 20007
(202) 333–9220; www.tvturnoff.org
Organizes annual TV turn-off week and materials to support
community efforts.

UNESCO International Clearinghouse on Children, Youth & Media

Nordicom, Goteborg University, Box 713, SE 405 30 Goteborg,
Sweden
www.nordicom.gu.se
United Nations-affiliated clearinghouse that publishes and
distributes materials about media, media violence, and children on a
global level.

VIDEOS/DVDS DEALING WITH WAR PLAY AND RELATED ISSUES

These videos are distributed by the Media Education Foundation, 60
Masonic Street, Northampton, MA 01060; www.mediaed.org.

Beyond Good and Evil: Children, Media and Violent Times

Examines how media shape children's ideas about good and bad, friends and enemies, and socializes them into a culture of violence.

Game Over: Gender, Race, & Violence in Video Games

Addresses how video games exploit gender, race, and violence.

Mickey Mouse Monopoly: Disney, Childhood, and Corporate Power

Looks at Disney's role in shaping childhood and the underlying stereotyped messages about history, gender, race, and ethnic groups inherent in Disney movies.

SAMPLE CHILDREN'S BOOKS DEALING WITH WAR PLAY AND RELATED ISSUES

Althea. (1981). *Desmond and the monsters*. Cambridge: Dinosaur Publications.
Baum, L. F. (1979). *The wizard of Oz*. New York: Ballantine Books.
Beckwith, K. (2005). *Playing war*. Gardiner, ME: Tilbury Press.
Cantor, J. (2004). *Teddy's TV troubles*. Madison, WI: Goblin Fern Press.
Carlsson-Paige, N. (1998). *The best day of the week*. St. Paul, MN: Redleaf Press.
Fox, M. (1994). *Tough Boris*. San Diego, CA: Voyager Books.
Seeger, P. (1994). *Abiyoyo*. New York: Aladdin Paperbacks.
Sendak, M. (1963). *Where the wild things are*. New York: Harper & Row.

Notes

Preface

1. *Who's Calling the Shots? How to Respond Effectively to Children's Fascination with War Play and War Toys* by N. Carlsson-Paige & D. Levin (Gabriola Island, BC: New Society Publishers, 1990).

2. This breakthrough in our understanding came when we found a very important 1986 article by Tom Englehardt in *Mother Jones* magazine called "Saturday Morning Fever: The Hard Sell Takeover of Kids' TV."

Chapter 1

1. This situation occurred not long after a 6-year-old boy in Michigan brought a gun to school and killed a classmate. It received extensive coverage in the news.

Chapter 2

1. See *Kids and Media at the New Millennium: A Comprehensive National Analysis of Children's Media Use,* by V. Rideout, U. Foehr, D. Roberts, & M. Brodie (Menlo Park, CA: Kaiser Family Foundation, 1999).

2. One survey of a mass-market toy store by Diane and her son found more than 200 products with the Power Ranger logo at the peak of the "craze."

3. Battling standards worldwide—"Mighty Morphin Power Rangers" Fight for Their Lives, by M. Lisosky (Paper presented at the World Summit for Children and Television, Melbourne, Australia, 1995, March 12–16).

4. See *Television and the Family* (Washington, DC, American Academy of Pediatrics, Revised 1999).

5. "How Violent Video Games May Violate Children's Health" by E. H. Song & J. Anderson, *Contemporary Pediatrics, 18*(5), 102–119, May 2001.

6. See *Media in the Home 2000: The First Annual Survey of Parents and Children* by E. Woodward & N. Gridina (Annenberg Public Policy Center, University of Pennsylvania, Philadelphia).

7. Gallop poll on public attitudes about efforts to control children's exposure to violent entertainment, released on June 23, 1999.

8. *Parents, Media and Public Policy: A Kaiser Family Foundation Survey,* reported by V. Rideout, Fall 2004, p. 15.

9. *Report of the APA Task Force on Advertising and Children* (American Psychological Association, Washington, DC, February 20, 2004).

10. "Companies Fight for Right to Plug Kids' Food" by S. Ellison, *Wall Street Journal*, January 26, 2005.

11. See *Joint Statement on the Impact of Entertainment Violence on Children* (American Academy of Pediatrics, Congressional Public Health Summit, Washington, DC, July 26, 2000).

Chapter 3

1. For instance, see *The Psychology of the Child* by J. Piaget & B. Inhelder (New York: Basic Books, 1972; Original French edition published 1966).

2. *Play, Dreams, and Imitation in Childhood* by J. Piaget (New York: Norton, 1951; Original French edition published 1945).

3. From "The Child's Political World" by D. Easton & R.D. Hess, *Midwest Journal of Political Science*, 1962, *6*, 237–238.

4. "Political Socialization and Policy: The United States in a Cross-National Context" by J. Torney-Purta in H. W. Stevenson & A. E. Siegel (Eds.), *Child Development Research and Social Policy* (Vol. 1, pp. 471-523) (Chicago: University of Chicago Press, 1990).

5. *The Political Life of Children* by R. Coles (Boston: Atlantic Monthly Press, 1986).

6. *War and children* by A. Freud & D. T. Burlingham (New York: Ernst Willard, 1943).

7. *Half the Battle: Understanding the Impact of the Troubles on Children and Young People* by M. Smyth (Derry, N. Ireland: Incore, 1998).

Chapter 5

1. The idea of taking our lead from the child in deciding what we do to facilitate learning is similar to approaches described in accounts of building "emergent curriculum" with children as well as in accounts of curriculum development in the "Reggio Emilia" approach. For instance, see *Emergent Curriculum* by E. Jones & J. Nimmo (Washington, DC: National Association for the Education of Young Children, 1994) and *The Hundred Languages of Children: The Reggio Emilia Approach—Advanced Reflections (2nd ed.)* by C. P. Edwards, L. Gandini, & G. Forman (Norwood, NJ: Ablex, 1998).

Chapter 6

1. The importance of helping children develop a sense of trust and safety, as well as a sense of control and mastery, has long been emphasized in theories of early childhood development. In more recent years, there is a growing body of work that points to the vital role experiencing safety and control play in reducing the impact of violence on children. For instance, see *Lost Boys: Why Our Sons Turn Violent and How We Can Save Them* by J. Garbarino (New York: Free Press, 1999) and *Violence: Reflections on a National Epidemic* by J. Gilligan (New York: Grosset / Putnam, 1997).

2. The "Safety Rule" was coined originally in a detailed discussion about how to put it into practice in *Teaching Young Children in Violent Times: Building a Peaceable Classroom* by D. Levin (Cambridge, MA: Educators for Social Responsibility and Washington, DC: National Association for the Education of Young Children).

3. *Bad Guys Don't Have Birthdays: Fantasy Play at Four* by V. Paley (Chicago: University of Chicago Press, 1984).

Chapter 7

1. From the *TRUCE Toy Action Guide*.

INDEX

About
the
Authors

Diane E. Levin is a professor at Wheelock College in Boston, where she has taught courses in early childhood education and human development for over 25 years. She has a B.S. in child development from Cornell University, an M.S. in special education from Wheelock College, and a Ph.D. in sociology of education and child development from Tufts University. She is the author of two books, *Teaching Young Children in Violent Times: Building a Peaceable Classroom* and *Remote Control Childhood? Combating the Hazards of Media Culture,* and numerous articles and book chapters. Diane is a former group therapist with emotionally disturbed children and kindergarten teacher. She is a founder of Teachers Resisting Unhealthy Children's Entertainment (TRUCE) and the Campaign for a Commercial-Free Childhood (CCFC).

Nancy Carlsson-Paige is a professor at Lesley University in Cambridge, MA, where she has taught courses in child development and conflict resolution for over 25 years. Nancy received her bachelor's degree in special education from Syracuse University, a master's degree in open education from Lesley University, and a doctorate in global education from the University of Massachusetts. She co-founded Lesley University's Center for Peaceable Schools as well as its Master's Degree Program in Conflict Resolution and Peaceable Schools. She has contributed chapters to several books about peaceable classrooms and global education. Her children's book, *Best Day of the Week,* tells the story of two children who use conflict resolution skills to work their way through a conflict.

For over 20 years, Diane and Nancy have been researching and writing about how violence, especially in the media, affects children's social development, and how children learn the skills for caring relationships and positive conflict resolution. Together they have co-authored three other books (including *Who's Calling the Shots?* and *Before Push Comes to Shove: Building Conflict Resolution Skills with Children*) and many articles on the influence of media and violence on children and conflict resolution.

Nancy and Diane are research associates at the Center for Peaceable Schools at Lesley University. They served together on the National Association for the Education of Young Children's Panel on Violence in the Lives of Children. They both have been recipients of the Boston Association for the Education of Young Children's Abigail Elliot Award for outstanding leadership in the field of early childhood education, and are co-recipients of the Peace Award given by Concerned Educators Allied for a Safe Environment.